Fair Exchange

Fair Exchange

A Ministry Exchange
Between the USA and Norway

Dell and Diane Shiell

Illustrated by Diane Shiell

St. Hans
Venice, FL

Library of Congress Catalog Card No. 91-67569
ISBN—0-9631376-0-3 $12.95

Printed in the United States of America

St. Hans

P.O. Box 1041   •   Venice, Florida 34284-1041

To
the members
of Gloria Dei Lutheran Church, Cedar Rapids, Iowa
and
the members and staff
of Den Norske Kirke, Larvik, Norway
and
to our three children, Bethany, Megan, and Ian

Contents

Preface 1

1   Coming and Going 3

2   With Pigs on our Decks 12

3   A Folk Church in Flux 22

4   Snakker Du Norsk? 45

5   En Plus En Er To 52

6   Bunad, Syttende Mai,
Holy Days and Holidays 60

7   You'll Love Yule (Jul) 75

8   Our Barn in Norway 86

9   Was That Lutefisk and Lefse –
Or Was It Hot Dogs And Lefse? 97

10   An American Priest in Norway 107

11   Over the Fjell and Across the Fjord 119

12   Yes, We Love This Land 132

Notes 143

Acknowledgements 145

About the Authors 147

Order Form 149

PREFACE

We have written about life in Norway and the Church of Norway as seen through the eyes of our American family. Our Norwegian friends often gave us insights into how Norwegians view themselves. Their insights and our own experiences provided our primary sources for this book.

We arranged our exchange through the offices of an ELCA bishop (formerly an ALC bishop), the Reverend L. David Brown, and a Church of Norway bishop, the Reverend Håkon Andersen. Between the time when the exchange had been agreed upon and when it began, the Evangelical Lutheran Church in America (ELCA) was formed and the Reverend Paul Werger became our bishop for the duration of the exchange.

The exchange was modeled after an exchange done by the Reverend Gerald Dyste from Farmington, Minnesota, and the Reverend Kåre Sten Larsen from Horton, Norway.

Our exchange almost died twice before we actually arrived in Norway. A letter from Norway confirming the exchange was sent to Bishop Brown and was lost in the mail. We assumed that arrangements could not be made in Norway and we gave up the idea of doing an exchange. We did not have the energy to start the inquiry and application process again. On a Sunday evening Bishop Brown called us; he had received a phone call from Norway. They had been waiting for a response to the letter that never arrived. A Norwegian pastor, the Reverend Sjur Isaksen, was interested in coming to the USA.

Soon after dates were set up and preliminary arrangements had been made with the Isaksen family, Pastor Isaksen's father was hospitalized for cancer. We had planned to start the exchange January 1, 1988. Rather than call off the exchange we proposed changing the starting date to April 1, 1988. Pastor Isaksen's father died, and the Isaksens were with their family in Norway for a few more months before leaving for the USA.

Sometimes prices or costs are given for comparison. They are usually 1988 prices. Allow for an average annual price increase of 5 percent, due to inflation, and you will have a more up-to-date price comparison.

Two families directly benefited from this successful exchange— the Shiells and the Isaksens. Hundreds of other lives on each side of the ocean were also affected. We are thankful to the many people who made this exchange possible. Our family dreamed of doing an exchange like this for many years; sometimes dreams do come true!

CHAPTER 1
COMING AND GOING

Our family experienced a ministry exchange. At the time of the exchange, our three children (Bethany, Megan, and Ian) were 13 years old, 11 years old and 10 years old. In the spring of 1988, we packed our suitcases—three each—and headed to Norway for a year. We exchanged cars, homes, jobs, and friends with a Norwegian family. We got the idea to write this book after we returned to the USA and began sharing our experiences with others. The Reverend Herb Chilstrom, presiding bishop of the Evangelical Lutheran Church in America (ELCA) commented on this ministry exchange in a letter to us: "I believe that a number of clergy in the church dream about doing exactly what you did through the exchange program."

A *Fair Exchange*—that is exactly what we experienced! Two families traded places for a year. Trading places, however, went beyond exchanging homes, cars, and jobs: we exchanged lives. Like most dreams that become reality, this exchange involved planning and work.

Two churches participated in this exchange. The American parish at Cedar Rapids, Iowa, Gloria Dei Lutheran Church, had a baptized membership of 550. Dell was the only pastor. The Church of Norway parish at Larvik had a baptized membership of 8,000. The Reverend Sjur Isaksen, our exchange pastor, was one of three pastors on the church staff at Larvik (a town on the east coast of Norway, 65 miles south of Oslo).

The first step in arranging this exchange was a visit with the Gloria Dei church council. We asked their permission to begin making inquiries into the possibility of an exchange. They gave their approval. Dell, then, developed a written proposal for an exchange and called this proposal an "application." This "application" was sent to our bishop in Iowa who forwarded it to the Norwegian bishop, who, in turn, asked Pastor Isaksen if he were interested. After Pastor Isaksen indicated his interest, he and Dell worked out the details for the exchange.

The following six guidelines were used for the exchange:

1) The duration of the exchange was about one year, each pastor being allowed to plan a month's vacation.

2) Each pastor was paid his regular salary by his own parish.

3) The pastors exchanged homes, cars, and pastoral duties during the exchange. Each family paid the utility expenses, car insurance, car and house upkeep cost for their own house and car. We sought a situation in which each family could have a home in which to live and a vehicle to drive, and the only expenses would be the everyday living expenses: food, clothing, and entertainment.

4) Pastor Isaksen had a knowledge of the English language. Dell did not know any Norwegian when he first applied for the exchange; he made this clear on the application. Pastor Isaksen stepped into a situation in which no one else spoke Norwegian. Meanwhile, Dell began to study Norwegian since he would be expected to preach and lead worship services in Norwegian; however, it was

obvious that Dell needed a lot of help from the Larvik parish. A committee was formed to help him with translations. The two pastor colleagues on the Larvik church staff spoke English and were very helpful.

5) Each parish formed a committee to get ready for the exchange and to help the pastor and his family get settled in their new home, church, and community.

6) Each family was responsible for the transportation cost to get across the ocean both ways. This involved a significant personal expense—the single greatest expense. Neither parish was expected to pay any out-of-the-ordinary expenses because of the exchange project.

We began our exchange in April, 1988 and concluded the following March, 1989. Afterwards we realized how fortuitous this schedule was. The children were able to attend school in Larvik for two and a half months before the summer break—just long enough to make friends and get settled. When they resumed school in the fall, they were really "going back to school" with its familiar surroundings and with classmates who were also friends. Meanwhile, the grueling pace and adjustments of the first three months in a foreign country were suddenly and pleasantly interrupted by summer. The weather was beautiful. We went on vacation and enjoyed ourselves. The rest of Norway was on vacation, too, so the pace at work and on our social calendar dramatically lightened up. When fall came, the whole family was refreshed and ready for the hectic pace of a new school year. How much better this timing was than it would have been if we had started in the fall! We would have depleted our emotional energy reserves, just as the gloom of *mørketiden* (the dark times) set in. Not even the typical *vinterferie* (winter vacation) would likely have been adequate to recharge our batteries. One needs to soak up all the heat and sunshine one can during a Norwegian summer to prepare for the winter.

It is important to mention something about the general attitude of the congregation in Cedar Rapids when the exchange was approved. We believe that the exchange was approved because the congregation cared about us. Though we emphasized the benefits of the exchange for the congregation, most people were excited about the exchange as an opportunity for our family. The congregation took the risk for us. Once the Isaksens arrived, the congregation grew to love and care for them. Then, the congregation also saw the many benefits of the exchange for themselves. Relatively few Gloria Dei members had a Norwegian background and no one spoke Norwegian. Now, however, many in the congregation are interested in Norway and the Church of Norway. The situation for the parish in Norway was very different. They did not have a voice in the decision for Pastor Isaksen to leave for a year and do the exchange; permission was given by the bishop. The Larvik parish learned about the exchange two months before the Isaksens left and we arrived.

Before we left for Norway Dell put together a notebook full of information and instructions, explaining how committees worked, who was responsible for what in the congregation, and what kind of normal activities were part of the pastor's responsibility at Gloria Dei Lutheran Church. There were challenges for both pastors. Dell had to learn a new language, but Pastor Isaksen had to serve as the only pastor for this American congregation. At Gloria Dei everything was new and he was alone to meet the congregation's pastoral needs. Dell helped to form an exchange committee at Gloria Dei. This committee helped the Isaksens become socially assimilated into the parish. The committee also facilitated a good working relationship between Pastor Isaksen and the church council.

By the time the exchange began, Dell had worked with our lay leaders to ensure a smooth-as-possible transition. Everyone believed that it was unrealistic to expect the Norwegian pastor to do everything Dell usually did. Officially, the only activity Pastor Isaksen could not do was to preside at weddings. The expectations and work done by our lay leaders and church members made the exchange possible and contributed to its success.

We exchanged jobs, homes, and cars for a year. We had to be ready on all fronts. Dell made sure all the pieces were in place at church. At home, the car was checked over and arrangements were made with a mechanic to do routine maintenance, take care of any car problems, and to send us the bills. Diane got the house ready to be someone else's home for a year. The closets were cleared out. All our dresser drawers were emptied and their contents were stored. A year's supply of vacuum cleaner bags was purchased, and arrangements were made with friends in case the washer or dryer broke down and needed to be fixed or replaced.

There was a lot of work and planning to do before we went to Norway. What do we do with the dog? This was our biggest question. It was difficult for us to leave our Sheltie at home. We ended up boarding her with a veterinarian who was a member of our congregation. Soon after we arrived in Norway, we received word that a woman came to the kennel and asked if any of the dogs needed a visitor. She "adopted" our dog, visited and walked her daily. We had arranged for the dog to be walked by someone already, but we never could have planned for the love this woman gave our pet. At first, we nearly said, "We will take the dog with us." Well, we could not do that. There is a four-month quarantine for dogs brought into Norway to protect the country from rabies.

The Norwegian family arrived before we left Cedar Rapids. The dog was still at home. The Isaksens' mouths dropped open when they saw our dog. We thought their reaction was strange, but there was so much going on as we prepared to leave, that we let the event pass without comment. After arriving in Larvik, a friend told us about their last evening with the Isaksens before they left for the USA. She said the Isaksens were laughing about all the crazy things that could happen to them once they arrived at our home. "Yes," they said, "maybe we will get there and find out they have a dog for us to take care of for a year."

We left the first of April. The middle of January, two and a half months before we left, Bethany fell in a sledding accident and broke her back. She shattered a vertebra, cracked another vertabra, spent two weeks in the hospital and another two weeks at home recuperating. She had physical therapy until the week before we left. The stress we felt was relieved by our thankfulness that Bethany was not paralyzed.

We did not take any electrical appliances with us. The girls and Diane took butane powered curling irons. They were popular in

Europe and refills were easy to get. The only thing we took that needed electricity was the computer which Dell used as a word processor. We had to find an electrical transformer for the computer immediately after our arrival.

Essentially, we took clothes for 12 months. We knew clothing would be expensive. We did buy some clothes in Norway, like Christmas dresses for the girls, but we did not buy a lot of clothing. Bethany got her confirmation dress in Norway, though. She was to be confirmed one week after we arrived home, so all of our plans for her Confirmation Day were made from Norway. (We had 30 people for dinner that Sunday in Cedar Rapids.) Her dress was a pretty white cotton skirt and blouse which cost $150 (three times more than we would have spent at home). Obviously, the Norwegian family experienced the opposite situation and enjoyed making many purchases. We took with us most of the bathroom essentials we would need for a year—toothpaste, contact lens solutions, make-up, and deodorant. These items were available in Norway, but the prices would have submarined our budget.

Certain ingredients went into making a "successful exchange." The two basic ingredients were:

1) two suitable parishes where the enthusiasm was sufficiently high, and

2) two pastors and families who were able and motivated to make the exchange work.

It sounds easy, but now we see how fortunate we were to have these basic ingredients "fall into place" for us. It is very important to understand that there were no existing channels or church structures to supervise and provide ongoing support for this exchange. The exchange pastors and their parishes were very much on their own. At the end of the year, we were all thankful for how well everything had gone. By then we all realized how many things could have gone wrong.

As great as the experience was, it was very tiring. Someone told us that living in another country is like playing football when every game is on the other team's home field. We worked hard to be organized, but we often felt as if we were missing a few pieces to a puzzle.

We planned, but you can not plan for everything. You work, study, prepare, and anticipate. What do you think was the first thing we needed after arriving in a new country? Milk? Bread? No, we knew those words. The first thing we needed was caulking and a caulking gun. Given years to prepare we would not have learned those words. The shower needed caulking and, after our showers the first night, there was water on the floor. So, early Saturday morning our first project was to find caulking; we had arrived Friday afternoon.

Our first shock was to learn that a wood-burning stove was our furnace. Never would we have thought to ask if there was central heat or not. The Isaksens thought it was so easy in Iowa to come home to a cold house, turn a dial, and soon the house was warm.

Sunday morning, less than 48 hours after touchdown, we went to church. Dell did not have a part in the service and all we had to do was show up to worship. It sounded simple and within the grasp of our jet-lagging brains. But...there were two churches in the parish. The plot thickens. We were told by one person to attend the smaller church. The congregation was expecting us and arrangements had been made for a newspaper reporter to take pictures of our family after worship. The morning was pleasant and we went home. On the way home, we saw some new acquaintances and stopped to greet them. We were told that the congregation at the larger church had planned for us to worship with them. They had planned a coffee fellowship after the service. We had not been told about the gathering because they had heard that we were going to attend the small church and they did not want to confuse us. We learned quickly that it was up to us to figure out what was going on.

After arriving in Larvik, we had to register with the police. We all had to have a TB test; Dell and Diane were required to have a chest x-ray.

Our third day in Larvik, we got a parking ticket—a whopping $50. We were suffering jet lag and asking ourselves, "What are we doing here?"

Dell preached nine days after our arrival in Norway. There was a post or pillar in the church blocking Diane's view of him. With her feet resting on the foot warmer under the pew in front of her, Diane calmly sat through the service, looking straight ahead. She had knots in her stomach and she squeezed the hand of one of the children. Sitting in the pew is always a powerless position for a pastor's spouse. You can not control what your spouse is saying, but here Diane could not even understand him. After the service, people came up to Diane, shook her hand, and told her what a good job Dell had done. Diane said, "Thank you," and smiled. She nodded and smiled a lot that year.

As we neared the end of the exchange and for our first three months afterwards, our feeling was: "We would not give up this year for anything, but knowing what we know now, we would not want to start all over again." Of course those feelings diminished as time went on. A year later the children said they would like to do another exchange.

Before we left Norway, we arranged for a series of small group fellowship meetings to begin soon after our return to Cedar Rapids. We used these programs to share our experiences (with slides, videotape, singing, and conversation) plus to encourage the congregation to share their experiences with us. We felt these events were fun and very important, even if we did them before we really felt re-adjusted to life back home. The level of everyone's excitement was very high when we first arrived home. After we had been back for three months, the project was completed for the congregation and it was life as usual.

We believe many people in the USA do not think of themselves as world citizens. About ten miles south of Cedar Rapids is a little town called Norway, Iowa. When we told people we were going to Norway, at least 75% thought we were going to this little town in Iowa (population 600). We caught on to what was happening and always said, "Norway—the country." Six months after our return, Diane was talking to two teachers at the children's school. One asked her if the children had trouble learning Norwegian. The other teacher looked puzzled and asked where we had been the past year. Diane answered, "Norway." The light came on. "Oh," he said, "I thought you were in Norway, Iowa, for the past year." Someone else we knew grew up in Korea. He was surprised when we said we would not see him for a year; it was just a short drive to Norway. Again, we had to say, "Norway—the country." This man was genuinely embarrassed when he realized what he had assumed. He said, "I should have known that."

Fresh flowers were part of life in Norway. It seemed strange in a country with such a short growing season, but then maybe not. The bright flowers on the table or the blooming plants in the windows added color and life during the dark winter months. Maybe they were essential. When we left our Norwegian home, farewell gifts of flowers filled the living room and it looked like a funeral parlor. The atmosphere felt like one, too.

Our last day was a Saturday and the kids and Diane were exhausted from crying. People stopped to say "Good-bye" and the children's best friends stayed around our home all day with red eyes. Their last "Good-bye" was around 6:00 p.m. when we told them that it was time to eat. Bethany's friend was upstairs with her and we could hear them both crying. Finally at 7:00 p.m. Diane said, "We must eat and finish packing. Annette has to go home." Talk about a heart-wrenching experience! What had we done to our kids? We all choked down some food. Around 9:00 p.m., the phone rang. Annette was crying. She said, "My parents say I can come to you in June, if your parents say it's OK." Life was restored to our home. Three months apart was bearable. We do not believe this was a quick decision to quiet their daughter at the last minute. We think some smart parents anticipated the situation and kept their ace hidden until the end.

CHAPTER 2
WITH PIGS ON OUR DECKS

We spent our year in a beautiful city on the sea. Someone once said that if you are having trouble keeping life's problems in perspective, then go to either the sea or the mountains. Once there, the grandeur of God's creation can give our problems a proper sense of proportion. Perhaps the mountains and the sea have contributed to the character of the Norwegian people. We often went for an evening walk and felt a sense of peace which seems to be missing in our society with its frantic pace.

Larvik has a distinctive European atmosphere with narrow, hilly streets, and older (but well-kept) frame houses with tile roofs. In the spring and summer flowers bloom in the yards, in planters outside of windows and on the balconies of homes. Plants bloom inside the home all year long on the window sill. Some of these flowering plants we were accustomed to planting outside in the spring. Diane asked a neighbor if it would be warm enough to transplant the geraniums and begonias. She was told, "No, they stay in the house. In the window they get sun and warmth."

We did have a garden, though. Norwegians asked us early in the spring if the Isaksen home had a nice garden. Since there was still snow on the ground, we did not know if they had a garden. "Yes, we'd like to have a garden this summer," we said. Strange looks followed. Of course we already had a garden. Confusion resulted because the Norwegian word for yard is garden. So, we had a garden in our garden that summer. We had rhubarb, chives, and potatoes. A friend started all the potato plants ahead of time for us. The growing season was so short that, even with this head start, most of our potatoes were quite small when we dug them up in the fall. To extend the growing season, some farmers cover their entire fields with plastic after planting. As the plastic ripples in the wind and reflects the blue of the sky, the fields look like lakes when you see them from a distance.

We did have a large back yard. There was an apple tree that we hoped would supplement our food budget; however, it produced only seven apples. The children had a lot of room to play, enough even to set up a game of croquet. There was no front yard at all. The house came up to the sidewalk and the sidewalk came up to the street. The kitchen window was on the street side of the house. People walking by could look directly into our kitchen when the curtains were open.

Our Norwegian home was located on a quiet street. Most of our neighbors were older, with no children living at home. They were not prepared for our children and their friends playing soccer in our backyard. The ball often made it over the fence and landed in the neighbor woman's flowerbed. Occasionally we saw her outside walking around speaking to no one directly, saying over and over, "Oh, my poor flowers." We felt sorry for her, scolded the kids, and made sure they said they were sorry. Still, the ball now and then made it into the flowers along her side of the fence. Not good PR. We told the kids that they were little ambassadors; they preferred to think of themselves as soccer players.

Typically, the neighbors spent a lot of time keeping up their yards and we tried to keep up ours, also. Our main effort went into just keeping the lawn mowed. A friend lent us a lawn mower he did not need because he lived in a townhouse. He brought us his push mower which gave us good reason to appreciate the short growing season.

After our first four months, we felt as if we had experienced four different seasons. The first of April we arrived to cold and snow. The rest of April was our short, cool spring. Then, we had a magnificent summer, May and June. We were told that Norway had not had a summer like that for twenty years. July was what the Norwegians called a typical Norwegian summer, cool and rainy. Because the potatoes in our garden were still flowering, we hesitated to call the end of July fall. The end of July and most of August, except for the first week, were cool. September and October were cool—typical late fall weather, as we know it. The leaves changed to bright yellow, but not to the vibrant fall colors we were used to. Megan and Ian were the first in our family to see snow that fall. In October, they went with their friends, a brother and sister, up to their family cabin near Rauland in Telemark— beautiful ski country. They awoke one morning to a white, winter wonderland.

We were told to prepare for November, the grey month; but November was gorgeous, with clear, crisp, sunny days. An older member of the congregation said he had never seen a November like that one. The first weekend in December brought 18 inches of snow. We were accustomed to snow in November and December, but this much snow before Christmas was unusual for Larvik. We started to worry. Our worries were unfounded. The weather was unbelieveably mild; it was the warmest winter on official records that had been kept for the past one hundred years. On January 30, it was 52 degrees Fahrenheit. The average January temperature is 27 degrees Fahrenheit. The average July temperature is 64 degrees Fahrenheit.

We had prepared for winter. We had "pigs on our decks"; that is, we had mounted the studded snow tires on our car. In Norwegian, a tire is a *dekk* and a stud is a *pygg*. Studded tires are legal in

Norway and are needed for driving on the steep streets and in the mountains. How else could people navigate on the steep, icy mountain roads? The argument that studs tear up the road is not very persuasive under those circumstances.

We were all thankful for the mild winter, but Ian and Megan were disappointed that there was not enough snow to warrant buying a *spark* for the children to use. A *spark* is a funny-looking chair mounted on runners—it is used like a cross between a sled and a scooter. One stands on a runner, grabs hold of a crossbar, and kicks (*spark* means kick) to gain momentum for gliding across the snow. You do a double-take when you see your first seventy-year-old whiz down the street, standing on a *spark*. There is a seat on the front and mothers strap toddlers on it and head to the store. They were very practical and added stability on the icy streets. It is a utilitarian winter vehicle, but to our children it just looked like fun. In fact, the children were more disappointed about the lack of snow, and not buying a *spark* to use, than they were about not going skiing (but do not tell the Norwegians).

It was Ian's job to bring in wood each morning before school. He made fewer trips because of the mild weather. The winter weather might have been mild, but the darkness of winter still came. When our children went to school in the morning we made sure that they were dressed warmly and that they had reflectors pinned to the front and back of their jackets and to their backpacks. They needed reflectors wherever they went those days; most adults did, too. When Dell and Diane went for an evening stroll, they wore their own reflectors pinned to their jackets.

The inside of the house was dark, too. We had brought solar calculators, but they were useless to the children when they left their math homework until evening. Before we left the USA, we were told that Norwegians left their lights on all over the house all the time because electricity was so cheap in Norway. The cost was probably similar to that of electricity in the USA. Most of the light bulbs we found in Norway were 25 watt, 40 watt, and 60 watt. That makes a difference both in how much electricity is used and how much light is in the house. Often lampshades were made out of cloth. When you put a cloth lampshade over a 40 watt bulb, on a very dark evening, you have a very dim room. If you turn on five of these lamps you still have a dimly lit room. On December 16, the sun rose at 9:15 a.m. and set at 3:30 p.m. In the northern part of Norway, on some days there was no sun or only one hour of sun. We were told that one starts to crave light. Perhaps that is why Norwegians leave lights on all the time. We asked someone who worked for the power company about this habit. They acknowledged this was a bad habit; they also said that the power company had the job of re-educating people to turn off the lights.

As with the low-wattage light bulbs, many of the household appliances were smaller in Norway. Before we left the USA, someone asked us if there would be a washer and dryer at our home in Norway. We assumed there would be, but the pioneer spirit in us said, "If not, we'll get by." There was indeed a washer and dryer, though some other homes did not have dryers. Our pioneer spirit was replaced by a practical spirit when Diane had to learn how to use her new washer and dryer. After learning, Diane's days often became dedicated to washing and drying clothes. A washer load, about one-third the size we were accustomed to, took about one and one-half hours to complete and the same to dry. Back in the USA, Heidi Isaksen summoned help from neighbors because of her worry that their clothes were not getting clean, since the washer ran only one-half hour.

In Norway, many items of clothing just were not washed as often as we were used to. Bedding and clothing were often hung out an open window to air out. Obviously there were no screens on the windows. The windows swung away from the house and were then hooked in a fixed open position. An occasional insect or bee flew into the house, but insects were not a major problem. We were concerned about birds flying in, but they seemed to know better. Fresh air is important to most Norwegians. Their windows stand open even in cold weather. Someone told us that fresh air at night is important; if you must shake snow off the comforter in the morning, that is OK. At dinner one evening, we laughed at this and told our hosts about storm windows. We said that all our windows were closed for the winter—we even cover them with plastic, sometimes. Their eyes widened with horror, and they asked, "Do you mean you breathe the same air all winter?" When we looked at it through their eyes, this suddenly seemed like a short path to the grave.

In Minnesota, the mosquito is jokingly referred to as Minnesota's state bird. Honestly, we have never seen mosquitoes in Minnesota the size of those we saw in northern Norway. The Norwegian word for mosquito is *mygg*. The children thought that the word was appropriate because Norwegian mosquitoes reminded them of the Soviet fighter planes called MIGs.

Living so far north, we had not expected to see so many mosquitoes, and we were not prepared for all the sea gulls, either. Of course, we lived near the sea, but in our mind sea gulls belonged where there were warm beaches, not walking on the snow in your back yard. When it rained, they perched above our back door. When we came home, we quickly ran up the front steps, jumped over the droppings on the top step and hoped we could get into the house without getting hit from above.

Our house was built in the 1930's. It was a white frame two-story house. It had been remodeled inside and was very nice. The entrance was on the side of the house. Inside the front door was an entry room with a coat rack. A door to the right led into the living room and dining room. The floors were made of wood, pine. We usually left the living room door open, but when people visited us they usually closed it behind themselves. Most people kept doors between rooms closed. We heated the house with a wood-burning stove in the dining room. The only way the heat got upstairs was through the living room door, past the front door and then up the stairs. There were no vents in the second story floors like we remember in our grandparents' two story homes built around the same time, back in the USA.

Also, inside the front door, past the coat rack, a door led into the kitchen. The kitchen had everything we needed, just smaller. The dishwasher was the same size as the one back home, but the stove and refrigerator were about half the size of ours in Iowa. The burners on the stove were flat one piece tops. One woman who had lived in the USA could not believe how inconvenient and dirty a coil burner was.

Microwaves were relatively new in Norway, but were gaining in popularity. Baked potatoes are not often eaten in Norway, but some people we met had visited the USA and learned to like baked potatoes. They had recently purchased a microwave oven and decided to bake potatoes in it. They called us on the phone when the potatoes were not getting done. Since the microwave ovens in Norway typically were smaller than ours back home, we suggested microwaving the potatoes for another ten minutes. After ten minutes, we received another call. The potatoes still were not cooked. "Should we try microwaving them without the aluminum foil?" they asked.

After using our microwave for a year, the Isaksens wanted to purchase one when they went back to Norway; we came home wanting a "real" coffee table. The piece of furniture that we considered most essential in a Norwegian home was a large pine coffee table. It was usually large enough for dishes, cakes, and sandwiches while having coffee. The Norwegians used this table for coffee-time. It was also great to be able to put a pizza in the center, sit around the table and watch a video.

In our Larvik home, next to the front door, to the left, a stairway led up to the second floor. At the top landing there were two doors, one led to the bathroom/laundry room and the other to the girls' bedroom. The bathroom was large. There was a sink, toilet, bidet, and shower. The toilet flushed by pulling up on the knob located on the top of the toilet tank. The kids first realized that there would be many surprises during the upcoming year when, after first arriving, they could not figure out how to flush the toilet. When American visitors toured our home, the kids disappeared when we got to the bathroom. They did not want to be around when the predictable question was asked, as the visitors pointed to the bidet, "Is that a foot washer?" In the bathroom were also the washer and dryer. They were placed on a small platform about four feet off the floor. To reach the washer, Diane had to climb a small ladder.

There were no hallways between the upstairs rooms. From the bathroom you entered Dell and Diane's bedroom. There was a large window with a scenic view. The Norwegian word for closet literally translates "cupboard" and the closets were like clothing cupboards that had been added to the house. The bed included a large foam rubber mattress, 6-8 inches thick, laid on a large piece of plywood within a bed frame. The bottom sheet, a light terrycloth material with elastic, fit over the foam mattress. The only blankets used were *dyna*, a comforter which fit into a sack-like top sheet. When it came time to wash the bedding, the outer sheet was removed from the *dyna* and washed. We were glad the beds were made when we arrived, or we might have spent a lot of time just trying to figure out how to make the bed.

From Diane and Dell's bedroom you went directly into the girls' bedroom. They had a pleasant room with bunk beds. It became a room for entertaining friends. Lots of giggling came from that room. Ian's room, directly off the girls room, was essentially a sleeping room. It had room for a single bed, a clothes cupboard, and one person at a time. So, Ian shared some of the girls' space. This usually worked, unless the girls each had a friend over and Ian was looking for something to do. The girls' bedroom had three doors, one to Diane and Dell's bedroom, one to Ian's bedroom and one back to the stairway. Downstairs, tucked under the staircase, was an extra toilet (or W.C.—water closet). It was nice to have two W.C.'s with five people in the house.

We have fond feelings for our Norwegian home. It had a super location. Back in Iowa, we drove everywhere; in Larvik, we could walk most places. Diane appreciated being able to walk to all the shops. She hates driving a car with a standard transmission which, once we arrived in Norway, we discovered the Isaksen car had. Traffic was crazy. Dell adjusted, but Diane always felt as if cars were coming at us from all directions. Before we left Cedar Rapids, Heidi Isaksen riding with Diane in the car, remarked, "Oh, so many STOP signs." Maybe we should have started to worry about not seeing a STOP sign for the next year. Most intersections in Larvik were uncontrolled, which left Diane white-knuckled. We did see an occasional YIELD sign and learned that the rule was: the person to your right has the right of way, always, even if you are on a main street. During our year in Norway, we saw only three STOP signs.

Shopping was done during the day, with stores open from 10:00 a.m. to 4:00 p.m. After the children's first day of school, Megan and Diane went downtown to get school supplies. It was 4:15 p.m. and every shop was closed. During our year, the grocery store started to stay open until 6:00 p.m. a couple of nights a week. On Saturday, everything closed at 1:00 p.m. and opened again on Monday at 10:00 a.m. When a holiday fell on Monday, it was necessary to buy everything you would need until Tuesday by Saturday noon. Before we left Norway, the controversy about opening stores on Sunday began. This controversy may continue for awhile. Everything was closed on Sunday. It will be unfortunate if Norwegians open their shops on Sundays; however, when so few go to church, the argument to stay closed is based on reasons of a leisure culture rather than religious reasons. While we were in Norway a small mall, the first in the area, opened in a neighboring town. This mall offered longer shopping hours than the familiar little shops. We realized we were witnessing a social change during our short stay in Norway. What did they call their mall? Downtown—in English.

Our two biggest challenges while in Larvik were the language and the economy. We had a hard time adjusting to the high cost of everything in Norway. Just to give you an idea: hamburger cost $5.00 a pound and eggs were $3.50 a dozen. Gasoline cost $3.35 a gallon. As a general rule, we found expenses for everyday purchases to be about three times as high in Norway as in Iowa. To be sure, this had a dramatic effect on us. Most of the money we had to live on, after paying housing and car expenses in the United States, went toward our food bill. Even then, we were always trying to economize. We mention this, not to complain, but as a point of information. We had heard that it was expensive in Norway, but we were not prepared for just how expensive it would be to live there. Still, we did manage, and despite the cost we were thankful for the opportunity.

The exchange rate and inflation were the causes of the high cost of living for us as Americans in Norway. For the Norwegians in the United States the result was the opposite, and their money went much further. During the period of our exchange (1988-1989), we received between 6.15 and 6.7 Norwegian kroner for our dollar. The average rate of exchange for the year was around 6.3 kroner. An exchange rate of 7 kroner and above would have made life much easier.

Another significant budget item was postage. Throughout the exchange, many letters and greeting cards were exchanged between Cedar Rapids and Larvik. We are thankful to family, friends, and members of the congregation who wrote to us regularly. As the dark days of fall approached, Diane sent for a correspondence course from the University of Minnesota. We worked hard to stay busy during the winter months. Even the children learned the lost art of regular letter writing. There was always someone to write to, and something to be mailed. If we needed a destination for a walk or a child needed a diversion, we headed for the post office.

Our daily lives were much simpler than in the USA. We planned our time and looked for ways to keep our days full. If we had an hour we grabbed a book, read aloud to each other, played a game, wrote a letter, or went for a walk. Most likely there was nothing on TV. Occasionally a re-run of "The Cosby Show" was on and we would plan ahead to watch TV for that half hour that one evening. A visitor from Norway was at our home in Cedar Rapids. The children were watching "The Cosby Show" and invited her to join them. She asked, "Are these the same children?" The kids on the show were so much older on the current episode than they were on the shows in Norway.

CHAPTER 3
A FOLK CHURCH IN FLUX

Religious life in Norway is influenced by a national history quite different from our own in the United States. Christianity in Norway dates back to the year 1030 when King Olav Haraldsson was killed at Stiklestad, north of Trondheim. Credited with securing Norway for Christianity, Olav was canonized by the church in 1164. Ever since, St. Olav has been the patron saint of Norway.

Stave churches dating from the 12th and 13th centuries have been preserved and attract the attention of tourists who visit Norway, and give Norwegians cause for national pride. By the 14th century there were about 1,300 church buildings and 2,000 clergy in Norway.

Catholicism lost its hold when the Reformation hit Norway in

1537. Norway, under Danish rule at the time, was declared by the Danish government to be Lutheran territory. A union existed between Denmark and Norway from 1450 until 1814. In 1814, the Treaty of Kiel required Denmark to "give" Norway to Sweden.

On May 17, 1814, Norway declared themselves independent and drew up their own constitution. The king of Sweden compelled Norway to accept him as king, but he allowed Norway to keep its constitution. The previous close ties that had existed between state and church in Norway were guaranteed to remain intact when the Norwegian constitution declared "the Evangelical Lutheran religion" as "the public religion of the state." Though Norway did not achieve complete political independence or national sovereignty until 1905, the constitution of 1814 served as the law of the land. According to the constitution, the king is the formal head of the church. Central administrative functions of the church are carried out by the Royal Ministry of Church and Education; i.e., a government agency. These administrative functions include the appointment of bishops, deans, senior pastors, and resident chaplains (assistant pastors), all of whom are civil servants. The Royal Ministry of Church and Education also issues regulations concerning worship and oversees religious education in the public schools. Church law is passed by the *Storting*, Norway's parliament. Church councils at various levels (parish, diocesan, and churchwide) convene to make recommendations to state and municipal government, as well as to give direction to parish activities.

Religious freedom was not won in Norway until the "Dissenters Law" of 1845. This law made it possible for those who left the Lutheran church to retain their civil rights, although they were still excluded from holding certain state offices until a constitutional amendment in 1878 and subsequent legislation. In the 1850's several religious groups became active in Norway, including Roman Catholics, Methodists, Baptists, and Mormons. The Adventists and others became active in the 1870's. In 1878, the Lutheran Free Church organized, independent of the official state supported Church of Norway. In 1906, the Pentecostalist movement in Norway began. All these churches, not supported by the state, were referred to as the "free churches." The Lutheran Free Church was the largest of the Norwegian free churches, until the 1930's when the Pentecostalists outnumbered them.

After 150 years of religious freedom, not very many Norwegians have given up their membership in the state church. The total membership of all the free churches and others (Jews, self-avowed humanists, Moslems, et al.) accounts for about 10 percent of the population. The major free churches today are the Pentecostal Movement (44,000 members), the Roman Catholic Church (21,000 members), the Evangelical Lutheran Free Church (20,000 members), the United Methodist Church (17,000 members), and the Baptist Union (12,000 members). This leaves about 286,000 other Norwegians who do not belong to the Church of Norway. The remaining 90 percent of Norwegians are members of the Church of Norway.

The Church of Norway is much older than Lutheran churches in the USA; one is reminded of this when one compares the age of the church buildings. In Larvik, the main church (*Larvik Kirke*) was built in 1677, about 100 years before the United States declared independance from Great Britain! The newer and smaller church building (*Langestrand Kirke*) was built in 1817.

One of the peculiarities of the state church system is the way that the government can make decisions about church property. Any church building over 100 years old is under the jurisdiction of a government agency which has authority for the preservation and use of buildings of special historical value. These buildings are not supposed to be tampered with and modernized, since this affects their historical value. Some Norwegians want the government to allow parishes to remodel the interior of their churches to better accommodate the needs of the modern parish; however, this is not commonly allowed. This government policy dramatically affects the life of the local church.

Back in "the old days" when these churches were originally built, there was no concern for Sunday School and parish fellowship events. Building space designated for classrooms, kitchens, and social halls was non-existent. Churches that have been built in Norway in recent times are usually referred to as "working churches" because they include space for these functional requirements of the modern congregation. The older churches, however, only provide space for worship.

In Larvik, the parish had recently completed a remodeling project. They transformed a crude cellar under the chancel into a small kitchen and social hall that everyone was rightfully proud of. Here, the church council met monthly, Sunday School was taught, and periodic fellowship gatherings were hosted. This remodeling project was not financed by public funds and was only possible because it did not interfere with the existing worship space upstairs or the exterior appearance of the building.

Typically, people have nowhere to congregate for fellowship before and after worship. The older church buildings are designed so you enter the nave, take a seat for worship and then leave immediately following worship. Therefore, going to church does not really help promote an experience of community among church-goers. People come and go as individuals, rather than as members of a faith community.

We heard some ideas people had for remodeling the old churches. One idea was to remodel the choir loft and/or the loft that runs the length of the nave. The main feature of the remodeling project would be the addition of glass enclosures so that these lofts could be used as nurseries for young children during worship. This suggestion very much reminded us of the sound-proofed "crying rooms" that one finds sometimes in American churches. In Norway, however, these rooms would probably soon be made to do double duty as a nursery during worship and as a place for coffee fellowship immediately after worship. The problem was that this idea did not enjoy much support from the authorities.

A more acceptable strategy, from the the viewpoint of municipal officials, was the use of old parsonages for needed fellowship and educational space. Many parishes were converting parsonages into parish houses. The proximity of these buildings to the church building (typically, they were walking distance from the church) made them well-suited to this purpose. Many pastors wanted to purchase their own home and therefore welcomed the proposal to put their parsonage to a new use. This scheme has one practical drawback, though; it requires people to walk from one building to another, sometimes as far as a block or so. As common sense indicates, once people have put on their coats to go outdoors, many of them are most likely to just keep on going home.

In all fairness, it should be noted that the government authorities are not the only ones who stand in the way of change with respect to old church buildings. The average Norwegian is extremely "loyal" to the old churches. People come in great numbers to celebrate the anniversary of the church which holds so much sentimental value as the "family church" where everyone in the family was baptized, confirmed, married, and buried. We heard that most young couples prefer their wedding in the "more romantic" old church instead of the young modern "working churches." You must remember that the Church of Norway is a "people's church" and when "the people" want things to remain as they have been for years, the church has a hard time to introduce change, especially when it comes to church property.

Among Norwegian clergy, one hears joking references to the debate between those who want the Norwegian church to be a "cathedral church" and those who want it to be a "coffee church." Apparently, the modern church leader who strives for more church fellowship space has fallen into the disreputable position of campaigning for a church where coffee and cookies are served.

While the local church building is subject to strict regulation, due to another curious practice, funerals are not held in the church buildings of the Larvik parish. In Larvik, the municipal cemetary had its own crematorium where most funeral services were held. Also, it was interesting to note that over half of all the funeral services in Larvik were not burials; they were cremations. The municipal crematorium was available to everyone in Larvik and virtually all the services were held there. We thought this was unfortunate because it discouraged practicing Christians from using the church for funerals. It seems to us that the church— where the community of faith regularly celebrates the sacraments and worships—is a more suitable place for funerals.

Other Americans who have attended a church service in Norway, Sweden, or Denmark often say something like this: "Can you believe how few people go to church over there? We went to a big, beautiful church and no one was there for worship on Sunday morning." We also noticed that worship attendance patterns in Larvik, Norway, and Cedar Rapids, Iowa, were very different! The churches in Cedar Rapids were full every week and those in Larvik were nearly empty.

The church attendance statistics for congregations of the Church of Norway are so dismal that we heard one American pastor suggest, "Norwegian missionaries should be called back home to evangelize Norway!" Very few members of the Church of Norway go to church; only an average of three percent of those who belong to the Church of Norway attend Sunday worship on a typical Sunday.

One Sunday morning while Bethany was out of town, Diane, Megan, and Ian were waiting for church to start. The children confided in Diane that they were genuinely afraid there would be only six people in church that morning. Diane then told them the story that one Norwegian pastor told Dell. He said that every Sunday before he left the sacristy to enter the chancel for worship, he prayed, "Lord, please let there be more than five or six people here today."

In Larvik, with a parish membership of 8,000, the average Sunday worship attendance for Larvik Church and Langestrand Church combined was 135!

We were told there are cultural reasons for the poor attendance at worship in Norway. For example, whereas Christians in the USA feel they must have a good excuse for staying home from church, Norwegians feel you ought to have a good excuse for going to church. More than once we heard "humorous" true stories of Norwegians who came to church only to be asked by fellow worshippers, "Oh, is someone from your family getting baptized today?" Another question asked of those attending worship was, "Have you been ill?" The implication was that if someone went to church, they must be near death. Also, an unfortunate attitude among Norwegians was based on the notion that those who attended worship thought they were better than others. This gave people a good excuse for staying away from church on Sunday: Others might think, "Oh, they think they are good enough to go to church."

A Norwegian pastor who had spent time in the USA observed that both Norwegians and Americans are proud of their churches. The difference, though, is that whereas Americans will bring their guests to church on Sunday morning to worship, Norwegians will bring their guests to church on a weekday to show them the building.

Another Norwegian pastor told us that Norwegians "both love their church and love to stay away from church." Obviously, one wonders, "Why is this so in Norway?" There are many reasons. One reason is that Norwegians love and value their free time. All over Norway, only a single worship time is scheduled on Sunday morning—11:00 a.m. It really does cut up the day to wait until 11:00 to go to church. We even found ourselves noticing a strange "empty" time of waiting between breakfast and when it was time to go to church. In Norway, Sunday is such an important leisure day that very few stores are open and there was not a Sunday newspaper to read before church.

One of the historical factors that affects church attendance habits in Norway dates back to an old law which mandated a minimum church attendance of once a year. This one annual visit to the local church was also the occasion for one's annual participation in the Sacrament of Holy Communion. This law is no longer in effect, but the habits it fostered remain very much intact. It seems to have become the standard by which most church members regarded the necessity of going to church. What is needed, now, is for people to develop a new habit of going to church. Some of our Norwegian-American friends have remarked, "Norwegians need to discover the habit of waking up Sunday morning and going to church because it is Sunday and that is what you do on Sunday." They might have a good point.

Another sociological factor can be cited for the current worship attendance habits of Norwegians. Norway has long been a rural society. With increased urbanization and migration from countryside to city, rural churches in Norway really struggle. It has been the case for many years that rural churches have had to share a pastor. The result is that churches are put on a rotation schedule for worship. Sometimes there can be six weeks between services in these country churches. Obviously, this undermines the habit of regular weekly attendance at church. The need is for parishes to devise some way to offer weekly worship. Since there are not enough clergy for this, the Church of Norway may have to give serious consideration to the use of lay leadership for these services.

Several Norwegians who did attend Sunday worship with some regularity wanted to make sure that we Americans realized that, in Norway, not all worship services take place in the local church on Sunday morning. Services were also offered during the week by the mission societies and public schools. In Larvik, an average of three funerals a week were held in the municipal crematorium, accounting for 150 services a year. Also, on Sunday morning, numerous remote "sports chapels" in the mountains and the forests offered worship for hikers, skiers, and others who flocked to the great outdoors every weekend.

Still, Norwegians face a gigantic struggle to reverse old habits regarding Sunday worship. A few months before our family left for Larvik, a representative from the Church of Norway stopped in Cedar Rapids to visit us. At dinner, our Norwegian guest (a pastor) told our children that they would not be going to church in Norway because if they did other children would think they were strange. This remark was not popular with Diane and Dell. Once in Larvik, we better understood why the remark was made. It was not uncommon for our children to be among the very few children at worship. Equally discomforting, sometimes Megan and Ian made up one-third of the whole Sunday School! But, needless to say, the Shiell children did continue the American habit of regular Sunday worship and Sunday School! Also, we were pleased to note that although our children went to church (and quite likely this was common knowledge among their peers), no one ever teased them or made fun of them or said anything negative about it. We can only hope that the Shiell children served as good examples.

This is not to say that we never encountered our own struggle to swim against the stream and keep up our worship habits. One Sunday morning a friend (herself active in a church-related youth choir) asked Bethany to go with her family to another town so they could go swimming. The friend called at 9:45 Sunday morning, as Bethany was getting ready to go to church at 11:00. It is not too difficult to imagine Bethany's disappointment at having to deal with this. Her friend knew that Bethany, like the rest of our family, always attended worship. But as we said, in Norway there is a very different attitude about going to church. Of course, this kind of thing put a bit of pressure on our family now and then, but we managed.

One of the two occasions when the church was packed with worshippers was on Confirmation Sunday. No other single Sunday morning worship service all year long rivaled the attendance on this day. Only on Christmas Eve did we see a similar outpouring of people for worship.

Something that seems to enjoy a growing popularity among Norwegians is called "Family Worship Service." Sometimes these services were held at one or the other of the two churches in Larvik. At other times, these Family Worship Services were held at *KUF Huset* (the YMCA House). Sometimes this kind of service was even held in the church on a weekday for one of the area schools. The distinctive quality of these services was the less formal setting for worship. Some effort was made to provide a more relaxed atmosphere. Families were encouraged to bring their children and the pastor often made some modification in the liturgy to be used. One such Family Worship Service was especially meaningful for us when Dell officiated for the first baptism to take place at *KUF Huset* in Larvik.

The Church of Norway is part of a changing society. Marriage and the family are deteriorating institutions. Inflation, unemployment, and discontent about taxes are on the rise. The population is increasingly relocating from the countryside to towns and cities. The homogeneous society of the past is struggling to accommodate an influx of refugees and immigrants. These and other social changes present numerous challenges to the Church of Norway.

The breakdown of the family perhaps is the number one problem facing the Norwegian society. During our year in Larvik, one-third of all infant baptisms involved children born to unmarried parents. A host of questions arise as the church lives with this social reality. The council of bishops, for example, has discussed whether or not the couple should be required to get married before the church would baptize the child. Some pastors do, in fact, take this position. As some Norwegian pastors point out, for a couple to live together and raise a family without themselves getting married is in direct contradiction to Christian teachings. How can a couple make a "good faith promise" to give their child a Christian upbringing when they refuse to base their family life upon the institution of marriage?

However, as one can easily imagine, neither bishops nor pastors share this position unanimously. Many ask, "How can the church hold back the Holy Sacrament and all its benefits from a child?" Quite likely, the bishops and pastors with the highest view of the importance of the sacrament also find themselves most burdened by this question. The higher one's view of baptism, the more certain one feels that parents must conform to their responsibility, and the more certain one feels that a child ought not to be denied access to the sacrament. Therefore, the same person often ends up agonizing with both questions as matters of conscience.

As the Norwegian society becomes increasingly secularized, the meaningfulness of baptism is easily questioned (as is the case in our own secularized society also). It is hard to know whether the request for baptism is for cultural reasons or for more specifically religious reasons. The state church heritage has made the use of religious rites very much "the Norwegian thing to do." So many are baptized, but so few are active members of the local parish. What is the church's responsibility in this situation?

The Church of Norway struggles with questions like this. In the diocese where Dell served, pastors were required to make pre-baptismal visits with parents.

Just how well-suited is the state church system to today's Norwegian society? Many prefer to think of the state church as a folk church—the church for all the people. To have a folk church is a wonderful idea, but how realistic is the folk church in today's secularized and pluralistic society? Norway is undergoing so many social changes.

Many of those migrating to Norway are not Lutheran; some, for example, are Roman Catholics from the Philippines. In fact, it is possible that most immigrants are not even Christian. The presence of Hindus from India, Moslems from the Middle East, and Buddhists from Southeast Asia puts a strain on the standard fare of religious instruction in the public school classroom. The increasing missionary activity by the Jehovah's Witnesses, Mormons, and various New Age cults adds to the growing number of non-Lutheran and non-Christian people living in Norway. Religious pluralism does not affect only the student population. More and more public school teachers (who are responsible for Christianity courses) do not themselves have a personal Christian faith.

While in Norway, we were approached by representatives of three groups who tried to proselytize us.

Our first such visit was with a man from The Way International who stopped by the house one of our first weeks in Larvik.

Our second encounter was with an American Mormon missionary who approached us on the streets of Bergen while we were on vacation. Though only briefly sidetracked from our sightseeing, this incident left a lasting impression: Norway is certainly being missionized by a variety of groups!

Back in Larvik, two elderly women came to our house from the Jehovah's Witnesses. They did not speak any English, so Dell talked with them in Norwegian. When Dell told them that we believe Jesus is God as a human being, they left our home in a burst of agitation.

Not only is the Norwegian society changing, but the Church of Norway itself is changing. The old state church system of the past is being changed by both external and internal pressures. Female clergy are not universally accepted throughout the Church of Norway, though the first female pastor was appointed and ordained in 1961. We read in the newspaper of at least one instance when government officials stepped in and appointed a female pastor to a position in the Church of Norway, against the wishes of both the bishop and the diocesan council.

Meanwhile, the future of the state church system itself is uncertain. There seems to be a growing separation of state and church in Norway. The church seems headed to a future of greater autonomy and responsibility for supporting itself financially. This is not to say that while we were in Norway, people were eager to talk with us about this subject. We were told that the issue had been intensely debated between 1975 and 1980. It had even been brought to a vote by legislators and church leaders. Interestingly, when the vote was taken 88% of the church leaders voted to continue the state church. Nevertheless, changes which grant more autonomy to the church are slowly taking place. Church councils are getting more authority for self-governance. With private funds rather than public funds, some parishes are hiring additional staff and building new church buildings. Still, the forces of institutional change seem to have gone "underground" for a while.

Years ago in Norway, many Lutherans expressed their dissatisfaction with the state church by creating religious organizations or societies. These societies came into being as the result of revivals among the laity. Many needs that were not being met by the church were met by these societies. In some ways, the programs and services of these organizations resemble aspects of congregational life and ministry in American parishes. They have their own buildings. They provide Christian fellowship, education, worship, and mission opportunities. Over the years, these mission societies have exerted such an influence on church life in Norway that, in many parts of Norway, their old antagonisms toward the state church no longer exist. In Larvik, the active lay leadership in the local parish were also those active in the mission societies. As someone told us, "If the Church of Norway of today had existed earlier, the mission societies would not have been needed."

In Larvik, we became involved with two of these mission societies, *KUF* and *Indremisjonen*. Both were organizations with good-hearted and dedicated Christian leadership. But, the question was, "How should the church and the mission society best cooperate?" The relationship between the two varies with each community. It seems that where a strong "working church" (the term used for the newly built churches) exists, the local mission society tends to become assimilated by the local parish. However, the more common use of older church buildings for worship and reliance on mission societies for Christian education, fellowship, and evangelism often detracts from congregational unity and strength, as members invest themselves in maintaining the mission societies as a kind of "church within the church."

So, amid concern for the future of the state church there is concern for two dangers which face the relationship between these mission societies and the church. On the one hand, if these societies pull their support away from the state church, the state church will more or less die. On the other hand, if these mission societies give up their autonomy and turn all their resources over to the state church too soon, and if the state ceases financial support for the Church of Norway, then the Church of Norway will not be able to turn to these autonomous mission societies for needed leadership and resources.

The Church of Norway has good reasons to avoid these extremes. First, these organizations have made an invaluable contribution to the history of Christianity in Norway during the past century. These organizations are independent of the government, the local city officials, and the local church council. This structural independence has been good for Norwegian Christianity and Norwegian church life. It has provided Norway with a core of committed Christians whose existence did not require official support, nor was endangered by official antagonisms. If members of mission organizations stopped going to church now, there would not be anyone left in church. Also, virtually all of the clergy in today's Church of Norway have, themselves, come from these mission organizations. Not only is this true, but based on the way things were in Larvik, that is how it will be for the future, too. If youth who are active in mission organizations like *KUF* do not become pastors, then who will?

The tensions that Norwegian pastors experience when dealing with the baptism of children born to unmarried parents are slight, compared with stresses due to the rest of the workload. After having been a Norwegian pastor for one year, Dell did not see how any pastor could begin a new year of service without feeling a tremendous need for confession and absolution. We were shocked by the sheer number of "contacts" in the community that the Norwegian pastor has every week. The nature of the folk church is such that the pastor is going to make contact with nearly everyone sooner or later. American pastors can become insulated from people who live completely outside the church. This is less likely for Norwegian pastors; although most Norwegians are nominal church members, they are church members. The conscientious Norwegian pastor, however, does not have enough time for a person-to-person ministry with all these people. There simply are not enough pastors in Norway to cope with the number of people who use the church's services.

Once Dell remarked, "When I think of the number of contacts that were available to me and how little time I had for each, I feel like crying." A Norwegian bishop replied quickly and sympathetically, "That is just what a lot of pastors do—cry."

The shortage of Norwegian pastors is the number one problem facing the Church of Norway. There is much more work to be done than is humanly possible for the number of pastors serving the Church of Norway. This is why many congregations employ lay catechists and deacons. They can relieve some of the overwhelming workload of the pastors. Deacons can help persons with special needs—grief support groups, the sick, the elderly, and the chemically dependent. Catechists can take most of the work of preparing youth for confirmation. Of course, there are certain areas of the pastor's responsibility that laity are not doing. Pastors preach and administer the sacraments. Baptisms, worship services, funerals, and weddings remain the pastor's chief responsibilities.

You might wonder if the government is more likely to supply the church with paid deacons and catechists rather than to provide it with more pastors. Probably not. That is why an increasing number of congregations no longer look to the state for these additional employees. Rather, they pay these staff salaries themselves. In the Tunsberg diocese (of which Larvik is a part), there were 36 paid fulltime catechists. Of these, only four were paid by state funds. The rest were paid by the congregations. This was perhaps not as common in some parts of Norway, but seemed to be happening more and more often everywhere. It used to be that no one believed it was possible for the congregations to do this. However, some congregations have shown by their example that the church can think of "paying its own way" without state funds.

In the USA, the average ratio of congregational members to pastors is somewhere between 350 and 500 church members to one pastor. In Norway, over 90 percent of all Norwegians belong to the Church of Norway and there are about 4,000 church members for each pastor. This disproportionate ratio of church members to pastors is unfortunate.

The average Norwegian pastor just does not have enough time to get to know the whole membership well. Church attendance is poor, but the pastor has no time to visit the 97% of the parish not attending Sunday services in order to encourage them to come to church.

In the USA, it is common for church members to expect pastoral counseling. In Norway, while the pastor does very many funerals, weddings, and baptisms, it is simply impossible to spend as many hours counseling individuals, families, engaged couples, young parents, and others with special needs as is common in the USA.

When only three percent of its members actually attend worship, it seems reasonable to say that a chasm separates the Church of Norway and its membership. The shortage of pastors makes it hard for the church to build bridges across this chasm. Parishioners are not likely to build the needed bridges, given their lack of commitment as a group. The state pays and little is expected from the people by way of direct financial support of the local parish. When little is expected, little is given. The way to start building bridges—as we see it—is to require a greater commitment of the people to the church, a financial commitment. The churches that seem to be pointing the way to the Church of Norway's future are those adding staff and paying for this staff themselves.

Although we saw negative results from the lack of financial commitment by individuals to the congregation, we had to admit that the financial independence of the pastor from the local congregation did have its advantages. Church members did not have any "say-so" about how much the pastor earned, since salaries were determined by rigidly adhered to national guidelines.

As a result, the parish pastor in Norway experiences more autonomy than an American counterpart who must answer to a local congregation that "hires and fires" its pastor as well as determines what the pastor's salary will be. Norwegian pastors also belong to a clergy union and (hold on to your seat) while we were in Norway the clergy union voted on whether or not to exercise their right to strike. The motion was defeated.

Perhaps you would be interested in the clergy salary structure, which was standardized for all Norwegian clergy. Clergy were assigned a salary level based on two main factors, number of years in the ministry and type of position held (assistant pastor, senior pastor, dean, bishop and so on). The following chart represents four examples of clergy salaries in 1988:

1988 CLERGY SALARIES
CHURCH OF NORWAY

Position	Years of experience	Base Salary
Assistant Pastor	3	$24,828
Assistant Pastor	10	$27,246
Bishop's Assistant	14	$29,421
Senior Pastor	35	$34,517
Bishop	35	$47,948

Note: A parsonage and utility allowance were provided. Pastors who received special permission to buy their own home continued to receive the utility allowance. The car allowance was based on the number of kilometers driven.

The similarities between the liturgy for the Church of Norway and our own in the ELCA are obvious when one has the opportunity to make comparisons. For this reason, we are concluding this chapter with the complete order of service for worship.

ORDER OF SERVICE
FOR THE CHURCH OF NORWAY[1]

1) Entrance Hymn[2]
MINISTER:
Dear congregation!
Grace be with you and peace from God our Father, and the Lord Jesus Christ. Amen.

2) Confession of Sins
MINISTER:
Let us bow before God and confess our sins.
CONGREGATION AND MINISTER:
Holy God, heavenly Father,
look in mercy upon me,
a sinful creature, who has sinned against you in thought, word, and deed, and who recognizes the evil desires of my heart. For Jesus Christ's sake be patient with me. Forgive me all my sins and grant me to fear and love you alone. Amen.

3) Kyrie
CONGREGATION AND MINISTER:
Kyrie eleison. Father God, have mercy on me.
Kyrie eleison. Lord Christ, have mercy on me.
Kyrie eleison. Holy Spirit, have mercy on me.

4) Hymn of praise
MINISTER OR CHOIR LEADER:
Glory to God in the highest.
CONGREGATION:
And peace on earth to those with whom he is pleased.
We praise you, we thank you, we worship you. Amen.

5) The Prayer of the Day

MINISTER:
Let us pray.
The minister reads the prayer for the day.
CONGREGATION:
Amen.
6) The First Lesson
MINISTER:
Let us hear the Word of the Lord!
CONGREGATION rises and sings:
God be praised!
Halleluia. Halleluia. Halleluia.
MINISTER OR LAY READER reads the lesson from the
Old Testament, or from one of the Letters of the
New Testament, the Acts of the Apostles or
the Revelation of John.
7) Hymn
8) The Second Lesson
  MINISTER OR LAY READER reads from one of the Letters
  of the New Testament, the Acts of the Apostles, the
  Revelation of John, or one of the Gospels.
9) The Apostles' Creed
  MINISTER OR LAY READER:
  Let us confess our holy faith.
  CONGREGATION AND MINISTER say the Apostles' Creed:
  I believe in God the Father Almighty,
      creator of heaven and earth.
  I believe in Jesus Christ,
      the only Son of God, our Lord.
  He was conceived by the Holy Spirit
      and born of the virgin Mary.
  He suffered under Pontius Pilate,
      was crucified, died, and was buried,
  He descended into hell.
  On the third day he rose again from the dead.
  He ascended into heaven,
        and is seated at the right hand
          of the Father Almighty.

From there he will come again
   to judge the living and the dead.
I believe in the Holy Spirit,
   the holy catholic church,
   the communion of saints,
   the forgiveness of sins,
   the resurrection of the body,
   and the life everlasting. Amen
10) Hymn
11) The Sermon
   The preaching text is read, followed by the sermon.
   The minister concludes the sermon with these words:
   Glory to the Father and to the Son and to the Holy Spirit,
   who were and are and will be,
   one true God, forever and ever.
12) Hymn
13) Announcements
14) The Prayers
   MINISTER:
   Let us turn to God in prayer!
   The minister leads the prayers.
   CONGREGATION responds:
   Responses to petitions vary. Most common response was:
   Lord, hear our prayer!
15) The Lord's Prayer
   (The Lord's Prayer is used at this time, only if there
   is no Communion. Otherwise, it is used later on.)
16) The Offertory
   (Typically omitted.)
17) Hymn before Communion
18) The Great Thanksgiving
   MINISTER:
   The Lord be with you!
   CONGREGATION rises and sings:
   And the Lord be with you!
   MINISTER:

Lift up your hearts!
CONGREGATION:
We lift our hearts to the Lord.
MINISTER:
Let us give thanks to the Lord our God.
CONGREGATION:
It is worthy and right.
MINISTER:
In truth, it is worthy and right
that we should at all times and in all places thank you,
   holy Lord, almighty Father, eternal God,
     through Jesus Christ, our Lord.
19) The Preface (changes with the season)
   Conclusion to the Preface:
   ...We join our voices with theirs and prayerfully sing:
20) The Sanctus
   CONGREGATION:
Holy, holy, holy is the Lord of Sabaoth,
   all earth is full of his glory.
Hosanna in the highest.
Blessed be he who comes in the name of the Lord.
Hosanna in the highest.
MINISTER continues immediately:
Risen Lord and Savior,
we worship and praise your holy name
   because you gave yourself for our sins.
Glory to you for the love
   which is stronger than death.
Grant us who come to your table
   to receive your body and blood
   that we may share this holy meal
     with humble and sincere hearts.
Unite us with you
   as the branches are united with the vine,
   teach us to love each other as you have loved us,
   and grant that one day we may be united with you
   in your perfect kingdom.

21) The Lord's Prayer
    (The Lord's Prayer is used here during Communion.)
    CONGREGATION AND MINISTER:
    Our Father in heaven,
      hallowed be your name,
      your kingdom come,
      your will be done, on earth as in heaven.
    Give us today our daily bread.
    Forgive us our sins
      as we forgive those who sin against us.
    Lead us not into temptation,
      but deliver us from evil.
    For the kingdom, the power, and the glory are yours,
      forever. Amen.
22) Congregation rises for the Words of Institution.
    MINISTER:
    Our Lord Jesus Christ,
      in the night in which he was betrayed,
        took bread, gave thanks, and broke it,
        gave it to his disciples and said:
      Take this and eat it.
      This is my body which is given for you.
      Do this in remembrance of me.
      In the same manner also after the meal
        he took the cup, gave thanks
        and gave it to them, saying:
      Drink this all of you.
      This cup is the new covenant in my blood
        which is shed for you for the forgiveness of sins.
      Do this as often as you drink it,
        in remembrance of me.
23) The Agnes Dei
    CONGREGATION:
    O lamb of God,
      who took away all the sins of the world,
      have mercy on us.
    O lamb of God,

who took away all the sins of the world,
have mercy on us.
O lamb of God,
who took away all the sins of the world,
grant us your peace.

24) The Communion Meal
The communicants come forward to the altar and kneel.
The congregation and choir sing hymns during the
distribution.
The words of distribution are:
This is Jesus' body.
This is Jesus' blood.
MINISTER (after the distribution):
The crucified and risen Jesus Christ has now given
you (us) his holy body and blood which he gave for the
forgiveness of all your (our) sins.
May he strengthen
you (us) and support you (us) in true faith to
the eternal life. Peace be with you!

25) Prayer
MINISTER:
Let us give thanks and pray:
We thank you, heavenly Father, for your gracious gifts.
We pray that by these gifts you will preserve us in
faith toward you, unite us in your love and confirm us
in the hope of eternal life, for the sake of your Son, Jesus
Christ, our Lord. Amen.

26) Closing Hymn

27) The Blessing
MINISTER:
Let us praise the Lord!
CONGREGATION rises and sings:
God be praised! Halleluia. Halleluia. Halleluia.
MINISTER:
The Lord bless you and keep you.
The Lord make his face to shine upon you,
and be gracious to you.

The Lord lift up his countenance upon you,
and grant you peace.
CONGREGATION:
Amen. Amen. Amen.
(During the subsequent time of meditation, the
church bell is rung three times in sets of three.)
28) Organ postlude

æ ø å
øy ære svøm
år møte lære
vær håpe rød

CHAPTER 4

SNAKKER DU NORSK?
(Do you speak Norwegian?)

After Dell initially contacted our bishop, we ordered language materials and began our introduction to the language. However, we really began studying Norwegian in earnest only after we were told that the exchange was a real possibility as far as the Church of Norway was concerned. Six months before we boarded the plane for Norway we were learning our ABC's and 1,2,3...

Dell requested and received the biblical texts on which he was to preach our first two months in Norway. He wrote sermons in English; these sermons were translated into Norwegian before we left the USA. When he was looking for people to help translate his sermons, someone said, "It always works best to translate into your own language." With that rule in mind, Dell found some Norwegians living in Iowa to help translate his first sermons. Sure

45

enough, later when Dell wanted to translate Norwegian newspaper articles for friends and family back in the United States, he confirmed this principle. It is much easier to find the words you are looking for in your own language than in someone else's. Surprise, surprise!

Having sermons written in Norwegian was not the same as being ready to preach these sermons in church. Dell's first preaching assignment was a mere nine days after our arrival in Norway. A translation committee in Larvik helped Dell with pronunciation of these first sermons. A considerable debt of gratitude is owed to this translation committee. The three committee members included: a nurse (who had a married daughter living in the United States), a high school principal, and a high school English and religion teacher. Each person on the translation committee helped Dell translate one sermon a month. (Each pastor preached three Sundays a month and had one Sunday off.) During the next few months, the committee translated sermons into Norwegian and made a cassette tape recording as they read the Norwegian script aloud. After Dell listened to the tape and practiced on his own, he met with committee members who listened to and corrected his pronunciation. During the last half of the exchange, the committee and Dell translated sermons together, and they eliminated the cassette tapes.

Others besides this official translation committee helped Dell. One woman met with him each week to help him practice his Norwegian. Soon after they started to meet they began translating *andakts* (devotions) and reading assignments from the textbook Dell used for his confirmation class. Other friends helped Dell with other translation projects, so he did not have to overload any one person. Dell's conversational Norwegian was acceptable for informal discussion, but for public speaking he wanted a respectable caliber of Norwegian. Due to the kindness and assistance of others, he was able to speak to groups with a maximum of self-confidence in an otherwise intimidating situation.

Language was a major hurdle and stress factor for us during the exchange. When we speak to groups in the USA about the exchange, most people consider the challenge to preach in Norwegian beyond what is reasonable. How many people enjoy public speaking in the first place? Most people, however, can identify with our children. Everyone has gone to school and remembers what it is like on the first day of school. One's imagination needs to go only one step further and imagine a classroom full of children speaking another language.

English is taught in the public schools beginning in the fourth grade. When we arrived, Ian's class had not yet begun to study English. Megan's class had completed their first year of English. Bethany's friends had studied English for four years. Bethany's teachers chose to communicate with her in Norwegian, but she had friends around to translate. Who do you think learned the fastest? Ian did not have a choice. He learned to speak from his friends and picked up the local dialect as well. By the end of our stay someone told us that she had seen Ian and a group of boys; when she had heard them speak she could not tell who was the American. What a compliment! All three children just accepted the challenge and enjoyed their school days. Their attitude was wonderful.

Someone said to us that for most adults, learning a foreign language is like a right-handed person trying to learn to write with her left hand. Bethany and Diane took an evening course in Norwegian. The course was "Norwegian for foreigners." They were trying to learn Norwegian with a class of 12 adults from seven different countries. Bethany was 14 years old, but by far the most advanced student in the class. She enjoyed watching these crazy adults study Norwegian. She gained help in grammar, but often she was entertained by her classmates. One woman in the class had lived in Norway for eight years and was only now learning Norwegian. She was from Thailand, was married to a Norwegian, and their common language at home was English. The common language used by the group for this course was English, also.

Norwegians often like to avoid confrontation, but we have a conversational subject to suggest, if you want to see someone get upset. One of Bethany's teachers speculated that twenty years from now English will be accepted as one of the official languages of Norway. Norwegian would be first, but English would be recognized. We tried talking about this subject once or twice and then decided to leave it alone; people did not want to hear this idea. It was not our idea, but sometimes ideas expressed by one's countrymen are not as offensive as the same idea presented by a foreigner.

We did not expect to find as many older people who spoke English as we did. During WW II when Norway was occupied by the Germans, Norwegians were not allowed to teach or publish in English. We did not expect many people over 40 to speak English. One group that surprised us was older men. Many men had been seamen when they were younger, and had traveled to many ports. The common language used in foreign ports was English. Many older women who others believed did not know English, spoke English to Diane. They would only speak English if there were no Norwegians around. It was not the same for Dell. Because he preached in Norwegian they assumed he knew more Norwegian than they knew English and spoke to him only in Norwegian.

Some people refused to speak English to us out of principle—we were in their country. Some people spoke Norwegian to us because they genuinely felt that their English was not good enough. These often turned out to be fun conversations for Diane. In this situation they would agree that each of them understood more of the other person's language than they spoke, so they talked in their own language, slowly so that they were understood. They would speak in one language and receive a reply or comment in another. In this way they spent an hour or two exchanging ideas and information rather than painfully groping for words to express themselves.

Some people believed that they were helping us by speaking only Norwegian. Others saw this as an excellent opportunity to practice their English as much as possible. Many of Bethany's friends enjoyed speaking English to her. She loved this, but her cruel parents often said, "Ask your friends to speak to you in Norwegian." Of course, if someone was comfortable speaking English to Dell and Diane, neither of them ever said, "Would you please switch to Norwegian?"

An annoyance during the early months was the children coming home from school confused. All three children were told at different times that they did not speak English. One day in school

Ian was asked if he knew the English word for *bil* (car). He said, "Car." No, that was wrong, the word was automobile. According to them he had not given the English word, he had given the American word. In school, students were given two lists of words, one American and the other English. We knew and used the words in both lists; i.e., the British say "sweet" and Americans say "candy," the British say "lift" and Americans say "elevator." Of course, some words were used more often by the British and others were used more often by Americans. Diane tried to understand this distinction that seemed so important. One woman tried to explain it. She asked, "What do you call the room under your house?" Diane thought of her home in Cedar Rapids and replied, "A basement." The woman beamed, her point was made. She took Diane downstairs and said, "In English this is called a cellar." It was a cellar! Diane's imagination was not vivid enough to call this a basement, but Diane lost because she had proved that in American one says "basement" and in English one says "cellar." There is an elitist attitude about teaching English with a British accent, also. American pronunciation is definitely second rate. Bethany's friends, who spoke excellent English, were actually reprimanded and there was concern about their learning American and using an American accent. With the burst of videos on the scene, they are fighting a losing battle. Children are now learning English (American) before the fourth grade from American movies. We never did convince people that English and American were not two different languages. Our failure seemed especially peculiar when we were trying to explain this to people whose own language encompasses so very many dialects.

In a homogeneous country of only four million people it is hard to believe there are two official Norwegian languages: *Riksmål* or *Bokmål*, a Danish-influenced language used by the townspeople and on the eastcoast; and *Landsmål* or *Nynorsk* based on rural speech. The children must learn both Norwegian languages in school and the hymnal used in the Church of Norway had hymns in both languages. Some people refused to sing if the pastor chose a hymn in the "other" Norwegian. Of course, they sang if the American priest made this mistake; he did not know any better.

Actually he was smarter than they thought and sometimes chose *Nynorsk* because the hymns were often easier tunes to sing.

Many English words for new ideas and inventions have become part of the Norwegian language. However, there are Norwegian words that became part of our daily vocabulary for which we do not have an equivalent English word. For that reason, initially, it was difficult to figure out the right time to use certain Norwegian words and expressions. An example of this is, *vær så god* (literally, be so good). You cannot survive in Norway without this expression. It is used everywhere, from the food you pass at the table to the package the clerk at the store hands to you. At first we had no idea when to use this expression. Here are some of its various meanings: here, here you go, please take this, please help yourself, you are welcome, please go ahead of me, and hello (when answering the phone). We decided it is an essential expression because it means so many different things. Another famous expression that is very nice, but had us stumped, is *takk for sist* (literally, thanks for the last). When you meet someone that you have seen before you say, "*takk for sist.*" You are thanking them for the last time you were together. It does not matter if it was a year ago or the day before. An interesting variation of this expression was used when saying "good-bye"—*takk for i dag* (thanks for today). One was thanking the person for the time spent together that day. Another gem is *takk for maten* (thanks for the food). Children are taught to say this at an early age for all meals—even if Mom cooked it. Adults use this expression also. *Takk for maten*—it eliminates unnecessary comments about the meal. Good or bad, the cook is thanked for the food.

We learned the proper greetings in the language books, but they were too formal and usually not used. *Morn* is used all day long. *God dag* (good day) always worked as a greeting. We also learned to say "good-bye." None of the books taught us to say, *ha det* (have it); this is shortened from *ha det bra* (have it good). It is the only expression we used for "good-bye" while we were in Norway. Dell sometimes used another expression, *på gjensyn* (see you later; 'til we meet again). However, the surprised looks that greeted him gave the impression this expression is either rather formal or old-fashioned. Several expressions are used for "thank you." *Takk skal du ha* (thanks shall you have) is common, but Norwegians seem to prefer expressing a multitude of "thank you's"—*mange takk* (many thanks), and *tusen takk* (a thousand thanks). A Norwegian word familiar in the USA is *skål* (skoal), an expression used when proposing a toast. A little background on the word: a toilet bowl is a *skål* and a dish on the table is a *skål*. Some people suggest that this expression goes back to the Viking tradition of drinking liquor from a skull.

We worked hard to learn as much of the language as we could. When we returned home Bethany was at the end of the ninth grade. We enrolled her in a college correspondence course in Norwegian so she could continue to learn Norwegian. The course was difficult and it took discipline to work independently. When your friends are learning French or Spanish in a classroom it is not as much fun to be studying Norwegian on your own. But, she continued to learn Norwegian.

Learning Norwegian was a challenge. We met the challenge because of the patience of many Norwegian people. They are a small nation working to preserve their language, but many Norwegians realize that as a small country their language is not spoken in other parts of the world. They have been patient with their royalty, also. At the age of two, King Olav came to Norway and began to learn Norwegian. Olav was the first king in about 600 years to speak Norwegian as a first language. We were not royalty, but we appreciated their patience with us, too.

Skole 3a

	Mandag	Tirsdag	Onsdag	Torsdag	Fredag
8^{30}		Norsk			Gym.
9^{20}		Gym.	Form.	Norsk	Mus.
10^{15}	Matte	Form.	Mus.	Mat.	Mat.
11^{30}	Norsk	Mat.	Krist.	O-Fag	Norsk
12^{25}		Krist.	O-Fag		
13^{15}					

CHAPTER 5

EN PLUS EN ER TO
(One and one equals two)

When we tell others about the exchange, a question often asked is, "How did the children adjust to school?" The answer is, "They thrived." However, as with many aspects of the exchange, it did not have to be that way. We were very thankful for their positive experience in school. When you take three school-age children and place them in a foreign country for a year, to be able to say that all three thrived is a blessing—it has nothing to do with luck.

The children knew we were thinking of an exchange very early in the planning process. It was a family adventure from the start. If one of them had said, "I don't want to go," we might have scrapped the idea. Each of us was risking too much, and it was not something we wanted to "talk someone into." All three children were instantly excited and said, "Sure, let's go." We admit that

52

when we first brought this up they were 12, 10, and 9 years old and they had no idea about what was really involved. Their enthusiasm was naive. Yet, as it turned out, their child-faith and excitement were warranted. Today, they are more enthusiastic about that year than they were then.

The children could not wait for jet lag to be over before they started school. We arrived on Friday afternoon. Monday morning, we registered the children for school. Bethany stayed at the junior high and finished the day with her classmates. All three started school Tuesday morning, four days after landing. The school officials on both ends—Cedar Rapids and Larvik—were wonderful. They did everything they could to help us and to make the transition easy for the children. In Cedar Rapids, we worked with school administrators whose attitude was that the kids would learn more from the experience than they would miss in the classroom. They were right. The kids gained much more than would ever show up on their report cards. Back in Cedar Rapids they stepped right in with the classmates they had left. Their grades did not suffer, even though they had been on a different track for a year.

In Larvik, the administrators worked not only to accommodate us, but to adapt for a "perfect fit." Bethany was placed in a class of kids one year older than she. Her age group was a larger class and the administrators hoped Bethany would get more help from the teachers in the next class. That class was perfect for her. We were thankful that people wanted what was best for Bethany and did not rely on rigid rules about age. Megan was in a class of wonderful kids her age and there were no special adjustments.

Ian presented us with a little challenge. The birthday cut-off for school in Norway is January 1. Ian's birthday is February 9. At home, he was one grade-level behind Megan. In Norway, he was two levels behind her. Megan was in the fifth grade back home and in the fifth grade in Norway. Ian was in the fourth grade back home and in the third grade in Norway. He was crushed and embarrassed. We said, "OK Ian, we'll ask if you can be in the fourth grade." The principal (rector) said, "Yes, if that is what you want, but first can we meet the third grade teacher?" We went to the second floor to meet Ian's teacher, and lining both sides of the stairway were all the little boys in the third grade class. As Ian approached them, each boy extended his hand to shake Ian's hand and to welcome him. What a heart tug! All the children in this class were waiting for the American boy to come. Ian did not want to be in the third grade, but when we left the decision "up to him" he decided to stay with this class until the end of the first school year. He would wait and change classes the next fall. However, by the end of the school year, these kids were Ian's friends and he never did change classes. An interesting thing happened; Ian is a very sociable person, and he became friends with many of the boys in the class ahead of him, too. Ian developed many friendships because of his dilemma.

In Norway children start school when they are seven years old. There is no kindergarten in the public schools. Since so many women worked outside the home and there were not enough day care centers, lowering the entrance age for school was being discussed. The elementary school is called *barneskole* (children's school). The hours of the elementary school day varied from day to day and from year to year. The younger children had short school days. Some days Ian would not start school until 9:00 a.m. and he would be home by 12:00 noon. Students at the elementary school did not have the same subjects every day, so the number of hours in school varied from day to day. The longest school day was until 2:00 p.m. In the sixth grade, Megan had classes from 8:15 a.m. until 2:00 p.m., three days a week and 8:15 a.m. to 1:00 p.m. two days. In elementary school, the teacher stayed with the same students throughout all six years. This has obvious "pluses" and "minuses," depending on the teacher and the class. The teacher got to know the students very well. There were no report cards in elementary school, only a narrative report at parent conference time.

Report cards with grades began in *ungdomskole* (young people's school). *Ungdomskole* was grades 7, 8, and 9. When grades were given in *ungdomskole* they meant something. Grades were taken seriously. A combination of grades and scores on tests given at the end of the ninth grade determined whether or not you would get into the high school you wanted. In junior high, the school day was from 8:15 a.m. until 2:00 p.m.; one was expected to go home and do homework.

In Larvik, there were three different high schools. The *gymnas* was the academic high school and was the track sought by students headed for college or university. A second track (the *handelskole*), for business careers, could also be used toward a college education. The third high school, a vocational-technical school (the *yrkeskole*), prepared students for the job market with a trade. It was incredible for Bethany to see her friends, at the end of the ninth grade, make career choices and work to achieve them. Along with the choice of high schools came responsibility. The students went to high school to learn, regardless of the school they had chosen. They had a lot of homework, but they had been doing homework since grade school. It was their responsibility to go to class and to behave with respect. If they were absent, or were asked to leave school, it was their loss. It was not the school's responsibility to police them—just to teach them. After the ninth grade the students were given responsibilities we save for college students. Most Norwegians compared their high school to our community colleges. If a student spent a year as an exchange student in the USA, they were not given credit for it. The Norwegians thought their high schools were that much better than ours.

At the end of high school, the *russ* (graduating seniors) of the *gymnas* and the *handelskole* celebrated for a month. Their fun was tolerated and maybe enjoyed by the rest of the Norwegian citizens. The kids painted old vans or cars and drove around yelling. They wore red or blue caps depending on which high school they were graduating from. They partied a lot and committed numerous pranks which were accepted. We heard complaints that the parties got out of hand and resulted in problems such as broken glass on the beaches and broken windows. These celebrations were a cultural tradition that went beyond "fun" in our opinion. Admittedly, we had never participated in these celebrations, nor were we the proud parents of a graduate. An interesting attitude of Norwegian parents was to put up with it. The attitude was, "Life is difficult and the kids should have a month of fun before they have to enter the real world."

At the beginning of the year each child was given a book called a *meldingsbok*. The student had to keep track of this book all year. When a child needed to be excused to leave school, the parent wrote a note in this book and it was initialed by the teacher. When a child was absent from school, the note was also written in this book. This was an efficient record of all communications, neatly recorded in the parent's handwriting.

Our children took all the usual subjects that we expected, plus more hands-on type classes than they had in Iowa. They had courses with generic labels like *o-fag* and *forming*. The kids knew what the courses were, but we had to work hard to figure them out. We think we finally understood. *Forming* meant courses of creative activities, including cooking, knitting, sewing, and industrial arts activities like woodworking. *O-fag* (*orientering* subjects) included social studies, geography, history, and civics. Another new subject in public school for the kids was Christianity. So few children went to church regularly, but in school they were taught Luther's Small Catechism, the Sunday morning liturgy, and the Bible stories.

In Megan's class a couple of children told the teacher that they were having trouble believing in God. The teacher invited one of the pastors to come and speak to the class. Megan was very impressed by this incident. Dell went to the school one day to hand out Bibles to the third graders. The pastor was always welcome at the schools. If Dell had a message for a junior high student about confirmation, he was invited into the classroom. A strange experience then followed—when he entered the classroom all the students stood up to show respect. This formal greeting was in contrast to the loose atmosphere usually found in a Norwegian classroom.

The relaxed atmosphere of the classroom was a shock to our children when we first arrived. During class the children talked whenever they wanted and it was accepted. After each lesson there was a break, which our kids enjoyed. Everyone called the teacher by his or her first name. There were no lockers and lunch was eaten in the classroom.

The students brought everything to school in backpacks. The junior high students then carried these backpacks with them from class to class. If it was raining or snowing and the children wore boots, they wore them all day—even if they were in junior high. As parents, we had trouble with this. We told our children to change into shoes so their feet would not get so warm. But they did not want to be different. So when they wore boots to school, they left them on all day. Our children were the only students who got a ride to school on some rainy days. They were also surprised to see that their classmates wore the same clothing two or three days in a row. Our kids never did start that practice.

We sent money to school with the children for milk, but there was no school lunch program. The kids took their lunch to school and ate at their desks. Our kids usually took a sausage and cheese sandwich with a top and bottom slice of bread. They were the only ones to eat this kind of sandwich; everyone else ate an open-face sandwich. By the end of the year, Ian was working hard to eat his sandwich, staring straight ahead. The girl next to him brought the same thing every day—an open-face sandwich with pink caviar. It made him sick. This kind of caviar was sold in tubes in the grocery store and was very popular. But, to be fair to the little girl who loved pink caviar—one day when Ian had a friend over for lunch, Diane made peanut butter and jelly sandwiches for the boys. Ian's poor friend almost threw up. He had never tasted peanut butter before.

We took so many things in stride that cause us to shake our heads now. We look at Megan's class notes for her cooking class and see that she wrote about the benefits of vitamin C—in Norwegian. Dell helped Bethany study for a science test about the skin, and she had to memorize the layers of the skin—in Norwegian. Diane helped Ian memorize all the counties in Norway and write them on a blank map.

One night Bethany needed our help studying for a geography test. We had never heard of most of the rivers and mountains in Europe that she was supposed to know. The children even had to learn to multiply and divide differently. Simple things such as writing the number 7 were different. If the children did not cross their 7, a math problem was counted as wrong because our 7 looks like their number 1. One day Bethany came home from school and asked us, "How many states are there in the USA? Today we were taught there are 52, and I raised my hand and said there are only 50." She was relieved to have us confirm that there are 50. It is easy to feel unsure of oneself in a situation like that, so we got out a map and counted them with Bethany. A similar situation came up for Megan. She was taught that there are five continents. We told her to ask her teacher about this. Then, we found out that they consider North and South America one continent.

The summer holiday, or vacation, was short. The children usually had a two-month summer break from school. The summer we were in Norway, the break was from June 20 to August 15. The last week in August, Megan's class went on a class trip. The sixth graders traditionally went to cabins in the Valdres Mountains (north and west of Oslo) to study nature. This experience was called *leirskole*. We were apprehensive about letting Megan go. Her teacher did not speak much English and Megan was only 11 years old. She wanted to go, but, on our Norwegian budget, the cost of the trip seemed expensive. We had just returned from our vacation and we decided that Megan would not go on the trip with her class. Someone in the community, (this person remains anonymous to us), heard that Megan might miss this opportunity. They contacted the principal and paid the expenses for Megan to go to *leirskole*. We were thankful to this person for giving Megan this memory. She had a wonderful time and never needed the wool long underwear she was told to take. She hiked long distances—in kilometers. She learned to tie knots and read a compass. She also learned first aid needed in the mountain wilderness. She learned all this in Norwegian. She learned to recognize the tracks of animals and feathers of birds—all with Norwegian names. She learned to identify plants, cones, seeds, and the trees they came from—in Norwegian. Most of the time it did not matter if she was learning in English or Norwegian because she was learning about these gifts of nature and their names for her first time.

During our short stay we felt like a part of the school community. There were several parent meetings for the elementary school; a high percentage of the parents showed up. As the first year ended, each class in the elementary school had its own program for their parents. Ian played the piano; Megan played the piano, also. Megan did not play for her class only, but for the entire school.

The schools were small, friendly, and casual. If a teacher in the elementary school was sick, the principal would often take over the class. She had a very good relationship with the children. If their teacher had a doctor or dental appointment, the children just came home early. Bethany had the unusual experience of being a Norwegian elementary teacher. In the ninth grade, the students had "work week," a week when they had jobs in the community. Bethany and a friend were third grade teachers for the week. One day the "real" teacher could not be there. Bethany and her friend were the only teachers for the class that day.

Imagine public schools without organized, competitive sports. Norwegians are very athletic people, but this is a part of their personal and social life. There were sport teams for all ages, with no connection to the school. The children worked extremely hard in physical education in school, and we know our children do not miss running up and down hills in all kinds of weather.

Norway is a small country, and Norwegians feel a part of the global community more than people in the USA do. Today all countries are dependent on each other, but not all large countries feel this dependence. Norwegians who had traveled to the USA often remarked on how difficult it was to get good international news in the USA. The presidential election of '88 was big news while we were in Norway. Norwegians were incredibly well-informed and interested in politics. We were often asked if we had voted. Yes, we had, via absentee ballot. They also wanted to know for whom we had voted. They usually were happy to share their opinion of the candidates. We often forget that the politics of the USA affect people all over the world. Norway touches Russia in the north. They were affected by Russia, also. The Reagan and Gorbachev meetings brought feelings of hope and joy for milder East-West relations. The school children learned a popular song called "Glasnost." It was a very moving experience to hear these children sing this song of hope. Our children learned much: new names for things, different ways of doing things, and the importance of accepting others and being accepted by others. We hope that even though specific memories will fade, the sense of global awareness and responsibility so strong in the Norwegian people will always be a part of our children.

CHAPTER 6

BUNAD, SYTTENDE MAI, HOLY DAYS AND HOLIDAYS

More than 3 1/2 million North Americans have Norwegian roots. Some of the cultural life of Norway crossed the Atlantic with the 800,000 immigrants who came to the United States between 1825 and 1920. As Scandinavian-Americans, we were familiar with some of the older Scandinavian customs. The traditions and social rules we observed while in Norway were a combination of the old and new being experienced concurrently.

At the conclusion of winter, everyone eagerly looked forward to *Syttende Mai* (the Seventeenth of May), Norwegian Constitution Day. In Larvik, everyone looks up the hillside to the Beech Forest and wonders if the trees will be green for the Seventeenth of May celebrations.

One of Dell's colleagues was quite humorous and outspoken.

He told us to prepare to see Norwegians become "hysterical" on the Seventeenth of May; "... much more than anything you see on the Fourth of July in your country," he said.

We knew that there would be an activity that included the children on *Syttende Mai*. The children came home from school and said that they were going to be in a *barnetog*. We knew *barn* was children and *tog* was train. The children were going somewhere on a train? Sure, why not? *Tog*, we eventually found out, also means parade. They were going to be in the children's parade. That made more sense, but we had already told the children they had permission to go on the train. Our American children marched in the parade on the Seventeenth of May chanting with all the other children: *En, to, tre. Hurra! Fire, fem, seks. Hurra! Sjue, åtte, ni. Hurra! Hurra! Hurra! Hurra!*

The *bunad* is the national costume that the women wear on the Seventeenth of May. Anyone who did not wear a *bunad* got dressed up. All the girls wore dresses and the boys often wore suits or shirt and tie. The men wore suits or tuxedoes. A Norwegian can recognize the county a woman is from by her *bunad*. There are 19 counties in Norway, but over 200 different *bunads*. Diane and the girls did not have a great longing to own a *bunad*. They were very expensive (around $2,000), but the value of the *bunad* went beyond a costume for *Syttende Mai* for a Norwegian woman. One woman explained their value to Diane. She said, "You never have to wonder what you will wear for a special occasion. You wear your *bunad* on *Syttende Mai*, to all baptisms, confirmations, and weddings. If you are ever asked to go to a dance to meet the king you know what you will wear—your *bunad*." What American woman would not enjoy having that fashion ace in her closet?

The children had almost feared the *bunad*. A teenager came to interview our children for the local newspaper. One question she asked was, "In America, do people have very many strange stories and ideas about Norway?" Bethany answered, "We thought that you wore the *bunad* the whole year—all the time." Of course they thought that. Before we left we had studied books about Norway from the library. Most of the books had pictures of *fjords* and people in their national costume. To the children a Norwegian was a person wearing a *bunad*. They were not disappointed when we arrived and they did not see a *bunad* until the Seventeenth of May.

In this century, when new Norway emerged as an independent nation, a loosely knit country was brought together. Previously, each community had existed with a life of its own; its own dialect, customs, building styles, superstitions, and *bunads*. These communities were integrated by modern communications and highway construction. Road tunnels, made possible by modern technology, were essential for linking regions in Norway. Norway is proud of their road system. The heavily traveled highway, E18, passed through Larvik.

As we traveled a stretch of E18 north of Larvik, we had the feeling that we were in a country with Big Brother Government watching us. Alongside the highway were boxes with cameras inside. We were told that, in order to catch and fine drivers who exceeded the speed limit, these electronic boxes monitored speeding cars, and took pictures of these cars, their license numbers, and their drivers (but not other passengers). Presumably, if you were caught speeding, your ticket was sent to you in the mail, and the photo was evidence of your offense. We were told that some people worried about the possibility that these pictures included the passenger seated next to the driver. Apparently, some people were concerned about the invasion of privacy; for example, when the passenger was a woman other than the driver's wife. This was not our worry, but the feeling of being watched, nevertheless, made us feel nervous as we drove past these camera boxes.

Norway not only requires people to wear seatbelts, but to drive with headlights on, regardless of the time of day the car is on the road. The law makes good sense, but what happens when you forget to turn off the lights after you park the car? The battery runs down. Dell kept forgetting, our first months in Norway. More than once the neighbors came over to tell us that our parked car still had its lights on. Other conscientious people would stop and come to the door to tell us about the lights. Later they would honk twice as they drove by, and we would dutifully go out and turn off the lights. The newer model cars are electrically wired so that the lights automatically come on and go off when you turn the key in the car's ignition. Our thirteen-year-old Opal was not equipped with this convenience.

In Norway, one has been able to buy a car without a government issued car permit only since the early 1960's. Now, all can buy cars, if they can afford them. The government requires a 100 percent tax on the sale of a new car. That means that a $15,000 car automatically costs $30,000 in Norway. A friend told us about the book value of his 1984 Mazda. His car had only 15,500 miles when he bought it for $12,900 in 1986 and this was a good deal. In 1988, the book value on this car was $15,300.

Stiff penalties for driving while under the influence of alcohol keep most people from driving after drinking any alcohol. We were told that the blood alcohol level tolerated is so low that one beer is enough to get one in big trouble. Excessive drinking and alcoholism were still problems in Norway. But, the threat of fines, losing your license, and mandatory prison sentences influenced most people to ride with a designated driver. While we were in Norway the law changed for determining the amount one was fined for driving after drinking. The amount of the fine was determined by the annual income of the person being fined. The newspaper publicized the fine of a man with a sizeable income: he was fined several thousand dollars.

We lived in a city by the sea and we would have expected drugs to be a problem. We believe that drugs were not a major problem. During our year, the authorities found drugs coming into the Larvik area by boat a couple of times. When this happened, it was a major news story, rather than something that happened often. It was the exception, not the rule. Alcohol abuse was Norway's number one drug problem. The commonly held belief among Norwegians was that either one did not drink or one drank until the bottle was empty or one passed out from drinking so much. The attitudes toward drinking seemed to reflect the traditions of Vikings and Pietists. (Pietists were persons known for their pious, "conservative" lifestyle.)

The family home was highly regarded as an investment in Norway. All Norwegians wanted their own homes, but the high cost of houses made it necessary to become very creative when seeking to become a homeowner. Something we noticed was the generation house. As parents reached retirement age, their children bought the house from them for a good price. Usually the price was low enough so there was money available to re-model or add onto the house so the older people could have their own separate apartment. The result was a house for three generations—grandparents, parents, and grandchildren.

In contrast to the high cost of living was a high value placed on leisure time. Everyone had four weeks of vacation each year. Because the summer is so short most people take three or four weeks off during the summer. Not surprisingly, Norwegians are the largest group of tourists in Norway. Almost everyone owned or had a *hytte* (summer cabin) in their family. Usually in July people literally "closed shop" and went to their *hytte*. Larvik was like a ghost town in July. Many summer homes lined the coast near Larvik and there were many campgrounds where people set up campers for the month. It seemed strange to us that businesses were not overwhelmed by the tourist trade. Practices related to vacation time were different—one just did not eat out. Cooking was done wherever people stayed. Even while traveling, food was taken along. A relatively new idea in Norway was to keep a week of vacation until winter, to travel to a warm spot. We knew many people, families and retired folk, who left for popular spots in Spain, Madeira, the Canary Islands, and Cyprus.

A deterrent to our fun at the beach was the Norwegian custom of topless bathing or swimming. We did not appreciate this custom at family beaches; it seems to annoy people at vacation spots in other countries, also. Many older people shook their heads and said they did not know how this got started or when, so it seemed to be rather recent. Most older people blamed the Swedes, but if the Norwegians learned this from the Swedes they learned this lesson well. Women would strip down to their bras at the beach or other public places if they were hot. Children were not expected to wear bathing suits until they were about five. In Oslo there were many women sunning themselves topless in a large public park where we picnicked with a Norwegian couple. We were uncomfortable and asked our Norwegian hosts if we could please move our picnic to another spot. It was interesting that many people who were against this practice were nonetheless defensive about it. We were told, "When it comes to sex you Americans think you are so moral, but when it comes to business you do it J.R. Ewing style."

Defensiveness struck us, also. One of the most often asked questions was, "Is it safe to walk on the streets in the United States?" The most common impression Norwegians had of the USA was the prevalence of violence and crime. Living in the Midwest, we rarely thought about the violence in our country. We resented being asked if we dared to walk the streets of our city. We lived in a city of 130,000 and always felt safe. Still, we realized how different our societies were when we saw parents routinely leave a baby in an unattended baby carriage outside a store while the parent was in the store shopping. We were shocked and realized we would not think of doing this in the USA. After this, we watched the news of our country differently and saw our society in a new light.

For the most part Norwegians seemed to be very pro-American. They were thankful for the help from the USA after World War II. Many of them had family connections to people in the USA. One area in which they have been critical of the USA is race relations. While we were in Norway, Norwegians were beginning to deal with race relations, themselves, for the first time. The issue became rather heated; often, in the paper, one group accused another group of being racist. In 1988, the year we were there, the government quota allowed 6,000 Southeast Asian refugees into Norway (national population 4 million). These people were supposedly dispersed throughout the country. Some people expressed the feeling that it was unpopular among some Norwegians to see the Norwegian government spend tax money to support people who come to Norway seeking asylum. The sentiment against asylum-seekers by some was expressed in graffiti we saw, in English, "Norway for Norwegians." Many people were dismayed that this racism was happening in their country. This slogan, "Norway for Norwegians," was disheartening to many in this country once occupied by the racially intolerant and despised Nazis.

From conversations we had, we assume that the average income for a household in Norway (with two people working outside the home) was around $50,000 a year before taxes. Taxes were high. People usually told us that they were paying about 35-40% for taxes. That sounds high, but not so high when we compare it to similar costs in the USA for similar services: federal income tax, social security tax, state income tax, health insurance premiums, deductibles and medical payments.

Norwegians were proud of their socialized health care system. Often when we complained about their high cost of living we were told, "Yes, but you have to pay to go to the doctor in the USA." They did have a comprehensive public welfare system for everyone. Many aspects of it were to be envied, especially for women. Many women were shocked to hear how things were done in the USA. They compared themselves to Sweden where they thought the women had it better than they did. In Norway, if you were going to have a child and you were working, you got six months off with pay. If you did not work outside the home you got $945. If you adopted a child you got four and a half months off, with pay. If you were a single parent at the time of the birth you got $1,425. If you had a home birth you got $225. Parents received additional money for their children: for the first child, $1,205 a year; for the second child, $1,281 a year; for the third child, $1,499 a year; for the fourth child, $1,595 a year; for the fifth child, $1,654 a year. After five, the allowance was the same as for the fifth child. Those who lived in northern Norway got $369 more per child per year. If one was divorced, the allowance was the same as if one had one more child. A single parent got $1,028 per year for the firs: child and $412 per year for each additional child, as well as the above allotment. Children received free dental care until age 18. This did not cover orthodontia. For each visit to the doctor one paid $7.70, until one reached a maximum deductible of $146. When someone died, the family got $615; the funeral cost was about $2,300. These figures are based on 1989 allowances, figured at the average exchange rate we experienced. They are used only to give you an idea of how their system works in relation to families. Their system is much more comprehensive. Allowances were given for many specialized problems and a transportation allowance was even figured for people who had to travel longer distances to the doctor for treatment.

There were more children who needed day care than there were places for them. Although the government paid a subsidy to those having children, the average family was not large. We knew quite a few young families with three children, but two seemed to be more common. Many women worked outside of the home and child care was needed. One of our friends was at home after the birth of her second child. Even though she was home, she continued to pay the day care fees for the older child so that she would not lose his place at the day care center. Day care center fees were based on 20-plus hours per week; 20 hours or 40 hours cost the same. For the first child, the fee was $385 per month or $18 per day. The second child was half the fee. Under 20 hours, one paid $2.30-$3.00 per hour. If one earned under $14,000 per year, child care was free.

Norway has a constitutional monarchy, but the day to day operations of government are handled by a parliamentary government guided by socialist ideology. Norway has a king and a prime minister. The Norwegian parliament is called the *Storting*. For centuries, legislative assemblies in Norway have been called simply the *ting* (thing). The Norwegian word, *stor*, means big. Hence, the parliament is literally "The Big Thing"—an apt description of modern government?

Norwegian socialism permeates Norwegian society. The gap between rich and poor is decidedly different from what we have in the USA. We got the impression that Norway had little of either extreme, most Norwegians belonging to a comfortable middle class. The tax structure and influence of strong unions seemed to have created a social climate in which we found a more dominant leisure ethic than work ethic. There seemed to be the attitude that if you did more than the least you had to do, you were only wasting your effort because you had to give this money to the government. Still, the typical young Norwegian family earned a dual income. The average work week was 37 hours and four weeks' summer vacation was very common.

The egalitarian nature of Norwegian society is met with mixed reactions. For example, the relationship between education and income seems increasingly to discourage young people from seeking higher education. Someone explained to us that if a youth begins to work at age 16 or 18 and works until age 67 (typical retirement age), they have greater earnings per their lifetime than someone who goes on to get advanced degrees and then does not begin to work until their middle or late 20's. Someone who begins an unskilled or a semi-skilled job at age 16 or 18 will earn more money before they retire than someone who studies to become a school teacher. The school teacher not only earns money fewer years, but also must shoulder the additional burden of educational expenses. Tuition at the university is paid for by the state, but most students leave the university with significant loans taken out to cover housing and living expenses.

Along a similar line, a fairly recent law (five years old or so) stipulates that graduates from all three high schools—*gymnasium, handleskole,* and *yrkeskole*—shall have equal status when applying for admission to the university. Previously, only the top 20 percent of Norway's students (the "A" and "B" students) attended *gymnasium* and then qualified for the university. Now, however, graduates from less academic high schools are supposed to be as readily admitted to higher education if they meet other eligibility requirements. Upon closer examination, however, there seems to be a gap between policy and practice. It seems that, in fact, graduates from the *gymnasium* are still more likely to go on to the university.

While we were in Norway we read an interesting statistic in the newspaper. Women are in the majority at Norwegian universities; they account for 54 percent or more of the students at the universities.

Our year in Norway was more than an exchange between the church of Norway and the Lutheran church in the United States— it was also a cross-cultural exchange. Not only did we develop a new way of viewing American church life, but also American domestic and international political and economic life. In Norway, so many people expressed their feelings of gratitude to the USA for its role in Europe during WW II and afterwards. Those days seem to linger longer and more intensely in the memories of people in Norway than back in the USA.

Also, it became apparent that economies all over the world are very closely tied to the American economy. We were interested in the daily fluctuations of the currency exchange rate while we lived in Norway. What struck us, though, was the realization that ordinary people living in other countries keep close tabs on the relative strength of the American dollar.

In Larvik, we met over a half dozen Norwegians who had been high school exchange students in the USA, sometime during the past 30 years. Others had studied at a college, university or graduate school in the USA. This contributed to a sense of fondness among Norwegians toward Americans.

Many Norwegians have relatives living in the USA, another good reason for those close ties and warm feelings toward Americans. Several of our friends recalled receiving care packages from their "rich" American relatives during the early '50's. The used clothing that had been sent in these packages made these Norwegian children the proudest and best dressed kids in town.

Often those who had been exchange students and others who had visited the USA as tourists cited example after example of American generosity, friendliness, and kindness. As those who have grown up under the gloomy cloud of the Ugly American Syndrome (associated with the Viet Nam War years), this came as a pleasant surprise to us. More than one person said that they were glad to show us hospitality as their way of saying "thank you" to Americans who had befriended them.

We found ourselves testing old stereotypes about Norwegian people and forming some new ones of our own. People also used our family to test their ideas and stereotypes about Americans and probably made their own adjustments, too. Sorry about that, fellow Americans. Norwegians often tried to tell us about their people as they saw them. Something we had observed was summed up by a friend as she tried to tell us about the Norwegian people. She said, "We Norwegians are solid people with our feet planted firmly on the ground. It just takes a lot to make us move them."

When we walked down the street people did not greet us—or each other. Eye contact seemed to be something to avoid. When Diane's parents—Rudy and Leone Schultz—came to visit in

September, Diane's mother greeted people she met while walking. The children had adjusted to ignoring people and could not believe Grandma was saying "Hello" to people. We have been told the Norwegians even have a phrase that translated "looking at someone out of the corner of your eye without them catching you looking at them." People tried to look at us without our noticing them. We often arrived early to church and the children and Diane would sit in the pew and look around the room. So many heads would snap forward as our gaze fell on them and caught them looking at us. We hope we did not cause any neck injuries. They were good people who probably would have liked to hug us in greeting or smile when our eyes met, but could not. In contrast, our friends often greeted us with a light embrace and the touching of cheeks—each side. This greeting was called a *klem*.

The children rather awkwardly adjusted to the *klem*, but immediately became comfortable shaking hands whenever they met someone for the first time or in greeting. When we entered a room of people we had never met before, we just walked around the room, shook hands and said our names, and they said theirs. No other words were necessary, just your name. "Mr. and Mrs." are rarely used, and men were often referred to in conversation by their last names.

The custom of having potluck meals did not come naturally to Norwegian-Americans. In Norway, when food was brought to a social event each family ate what they brought. When we were invited to group meetings our first spring in Norway there were always designated hosts who brought food for themselves and us. Afterwards we learned to bring our own *smørbrød* and cake, if Dell was not the guest speaker. Sometimes cakes and coffee were shared after a church service. These social events were not as frequent as our church coffee hour in the USA. The reason, we felt, was the formal nature of these events in Norway. When we first arrived we were extremely impressed. We thought, "Now this is the way we should do it back home. Here is the lost art of socializing." But, the practical Americans changed their tune over time. Coffee was served in "real" coffee cups with saucers, plates, on cloth tablecloths, with lit candles, and fresh cut flowers. It was extremely nice, but what about the women who had to prepare this and clean up? Often the same women had to do this over and over and were not too happy about it. There must be a middle ground between using styrofoam cups and using cups that one or two people must wash. Our simpler coffee fellowship times back in the States may lack some elegance, but the important thing is that they keep happening regularly.

In November, Bethany came home and said, "Hey everybody, guess what! I heard a Norwegian say *uff da*!" In Minnesota, this expression is so familiar, and so distinctly Scandinavian-American, that T-shirts and other novelty items have "*uff da*" printed on them. The *Norwegian-English Dictionary* offers this definition for *uff da*: "oo, oof, ugh; oh dear...; expresses unpleasant feelings, e.g. alarm, uneasiness, aversion, disgust, irritation, regret."[3] Just as reassuring to us was to see that slimy, lye-soaked cod (*lutefisk*) appear in the fishshop and disappear each day. Younger people tried to tell us that eating this delicacy was dead, and only Norwegian-Americans ate it, but we can cling to our belief that Norwegians still eat *lutefisk*, because someone was buying it. At least some of our myths were restored.

And what do Americans eat? We had an American night at the *KUF Huset* or the YMCA building. Our family provided the program and afterward we were all treated to a truly "American" meal planned by a committee. We ate corn-on-the-cob and white bread. The corn-on-the-cob was sold in cans at the local grocery store. We demonstrated how to butter and salt it liberally and how to pick it up to eat it. So, our typical American meal, according to our Norwegian friends, was corn-on-the-cob and white bread. It is interesting how others see us.

KUF raised money each fall and spring by means of a *løppemarked* or flea market. We never saw a garage sale in Norway, but they had heard about them. Most Norwegians did not have garages, but that was not why we did not see garage sales. Some people told Diane that they envied the bold Americans who sold their used items for a profit. They did not think that they could put their used items out to be sold without being embarrassed and having others think they were poor. So, they ended up donating their used items to charity groups. *KUF* often received a lot of these goods for their flea market.

The animosity between the Swedes and Norwegians is material for many jokes in Minnesota and other places. We found that it was not original to Minnesota. It happens in Norway and Sweden, too. Diane's great-grandparents came to the USA from Sweden. Our family looked more Norwegian than most Norwegian families, so we were often asked if our family's roots were Norwegian. Dell could say "Yes," but Diane had to admit to being Swedish and German. People genuinely felt sorry for her. They would say "Ohhhhh" (with the 'too bad' understood). While we were in Sweden at Diane's relatives' house, the children got to try the Swedish version of Norwegian skiing. On the grass was a pair of skis with three sets of straps to slide your feet into. Everyone encouraged the children to try them. Our three children put on the one pair of skis. Then they tried to move forward in a coordinated effort on the grass. Sound easy? You must be Swedish. Our children toppled from side to side and entertained our Swedish family.

In Norway, religious "holy days" have become secular "holidays." True, there are worship services on holy days, but few people actually attend these services. Most people have the day off and leave town. The most glaring example of this is Easter. How does the church compete with a cultural holiday time that even has its own vocabulary? Easter is vacation time. In fact, the word for Easter vacation is *påske ferie*, but another specific word, *påske tur*, means Easter vacation to the mountains to ski. The whole nation leaves town to ski. You drive in *påske traffik*—Easter traffic of vacationers. On your trip you get *påske brun*—a tan from Easter vacation in the mountains. Once, Diane commented that it would be nice if people went to church on Easter. A woman tried to explain why people had to be out of town at Eastertime. She said that anyone from the mountains would not feel right being by the sea at Eastertime; most Norwegians felt that they must go to the mountains. Most Norwegian-Americans must have lost this instinct.

Easter is not the only "holy day" which has become a Norwegian holiday. The same goes for numerous other holy days like the day after Christmas (the second day of Christmas), the Monday after

Pentecost (Whitmonday), and All Saints Day. Services were held at church, but very few attended.

Ascension Day is also on our liturgical calendar in the USA—40 days after Easter. It always falls on a Thursday and is not usually observed with a service in the USA. In Norway, this day, called *Kristi Himmelfartsdagen*, is observed as a day off and services are held at the church.

Though not a "holy day" as such, May 8 is celebrated as the day Norwegians won freedom from Nazi occupation during World War II. In Oslo, one may visit the Resistance Museum where tribute is paid to Norwegians who died while resisting the Nazis.

One of Norway's holy days is St. Olav Day (July 29). This is the day that Viking King Olav is honored. King Olav is credited with making Norway a Christian nation. King Olav died in 1030. After he died, legend has it that his hair and nails continued to grow. Later, he was sainted.

Another holy day is St. John the Baptist Day (St. Hans, also known as Midsummer's Day and Eve). This holy day is designated as June 24, the longest day of the year, but is celebrated the night before, June 23. We were reminded of the religious significance of this day. John the Baptist said, "I must decrease" and Jesus "must increase." After Christmas, the days keep getting longer and longer, until June 24. Then, the days get shorter and shorter, until the next Christmas. As with many holy days, one can read of both Christian and pre-Christian explanations for these celebrations. In Norway, this celebration of the shortest night and the longest day dates back to pre-Christian times when bonfires were lit to signify the defeat of darkness and to celebrate the power of the sungod.

We celebrated the "longest day of the year" near Sandefjord, at *Knattholmen*, a Scout Camp owned by *KFUK/KFUM* (the Norwegian YWCA/YMCA). The weather was great. We had a picnic and were entertained by a delightful outdoor program. There were musicians, a magician and a couple hundred adults and children. It was too dry for the traditional St. Hans Day bonfire on the *fjord* beach. We were told that it had been "about 100 years" since they had not been able to have a bonfire as part of this celebration. As we drove back to Larvik, around midnight, it was still light outside.

We noticed how long the days were throughout June. At night, we had trouble getting to sleep before 11:00 or 11:30. It was so light outside! We were thankful that the Isaksens had bought darkening window shades for the bedrooms, before they left for the USA. It probably would have been impossible to sleep without them. We were told that Norwegians do not mind the impossibility of sleep during the long days of June and early July. They have so many dark days through fall and winter that they literally crave the sun and want to get all they can before fall begins again. Around the middle of August, we noticed the days getting shorter. Eventually, we ourselves came to crave sunshine.

In the fall, United Nations Week was celebrated throughout Norway with numerous festivities. A church service was held in the Larvik Church to celebrate Norway as a "colorful society"— a powerful counterstatement to those who used the slogan, "Norway for Norwegians!"

During a visit to the nursing home, Dell was told by a resident that October 14 is "winter day," the first day of winter in Norway. Our October 14 provided us a hard frost overnight. The daytime temperature was around 40 degrees Fahrenheit.

We wonder how many young Norwegians today know that October 14 is "winter day." Beliefs, values, and social rules change slowly in a country where your neighbor looks somewhat like you, belongs to the same church, shares most of your cultural traditions and a similar history. Change comes slowly in Norway, but change does come.

CHAPTER 7
YOU'LL LOVE YULE (JUL)

As Christmas approached, people in Larvik often told us how happy they were that we would be in Norway for a Norwegian Christmas. Because of our Scandinavian heritage we believed that we would get a pure version of our celebrations back home. To some extent this was true, we were familiar with some of the customs. Their Christmas was a very joyous season that combined the religious and secular aspects. Traditional preparations and religious services filled the days. Christmas dominated the days of December and continued into January. There was a simplicity in preparing for Christmas that we have lost. We understand now why our friends wanted us to experience a Norwegian Christmas.

This might boggle the minds of some, but the Christmas season did not start until December. Once December came, the preparations and celebrations were intense. Intense but focused. Everything during this season was Christmas. The Norwegian word for Christmas is *Jul*. Everything advertized was now *Jul-* something or other. An ad for a broom would now be, "Buy your *julekost* (Christmas broom)." Packages for food were decorated with Christmas scenes. All the milk cartons had colorful scenes printed on them. Even the anchovies came in colorful tins and were called *juleansjos* (Christmas anchovies). Every group—secular and religious—had a Christmas celebration. For us, December was exciting, magical, and stressful. The church was very important at Christmastime. It is also important to have a priest or pastor at your Christmas celebration. Whom should we invite? The American Priest! It was an honor of course, but Dell sometimes felt as if the Christmas Season was something he survived.

The church building was used extensively during December. The calendar was full of Christmas concerts by community bands and choirs. All of the Larvik schools had Christmas programs and worship services in the church. The pastors supervised the preparations for these programs. The children walked from the schools to the church. All the schools had their services at different times. Diane attended three services for the Larvik schools. Megan and Ian were in the elementary program, Bethany was in the junior high program, and Dell had helped plan the high school program. It was a very stirring experience to see all these school children together in church celebrating the real meaning of Christmas with their classmates and teachers. It was one of those many times during the year when our criticism about the absence of youth in church sounded hollow. We felt sad that our children had grown up in the USA singing "Jolly Old Saint Nicholas" and "Rudolph the Red Nosed Reindeer" with their school friends during the Christmas season instead of singing carols and hearing scripture readings.

Another December holiday was Santa Lucia Day. The Norwegians borrowed this celebration from the Swedes, but it is their holiday now, too. The children in Ian's class had a special program and one of Bethany's classes went to nursing homes to sing. Bethany was chosen to be Santa Lucia. She wore a white robe with a red sash, and a crown of lighted candles. The girls in Bethany's class had baked treats and offered these to the nursing home residents. This was in keeping with the legend that Lucia distributed food to people in Sweden who were starving during a great famine. They also sang Christmas carols. This was the nearest we came to seeing any activity that resembled Christmas caroling.

It makes sense that the Norwegians have adopted this holiday. Santa Lucia's name means "light." In both Sweden and Norway light was important on December 13 which was the shortest day of the year before calendar reform. Santa Lucia was the "light saint" who signaled an end to their long, dark winter nights. For the church she is also a symbol of light. She comes in the middle of Advent as a reflection of the Light of the World who comes on Christmas Day. According to one legend, Lucia was a Christian girl who lived centuries ago in Rome. She refused to give up her religion to marry a pagan and was to be burned at the stake. The flames were around her, but did not burn her, so a sword was plunged into her heart. The song, sung on her day, speaks of the dark winter night and Santa Lucia bringing cheer with her crown of light. The custom on December 13 in Scandinavian homes is for a girl in a white dress and wearing a wreath with burning candles, to awaken the family from sleep and offer a tray of coffee and cakes.

A Norwegian Christmas includes special work projects around the house. One tradition requires a special housecleaning effort during the second week of Advent. After a thorough scrubbing of walls, ceilings, and furniture the smell of "greensoap" (a thick cleaning detergent with a distinctive aroma) fills the air in each Norwegian home. Doesn't that sound like a nice tradition? It is, but we got the impression that the belief of what is a tradition dies much harder than the actual practice of the tradition! No doubt many still clean house this way, but one cannot ignore the number of younger women who simply won't because they are too tired when they come home from work.

Do the younger women keep the tradition of baking seven kinds of Christmas cookies? One wonders. Some older Norwegians told us that "fourteen" (not seven) was the traditional number of special cookies one ought to bake right before Christmas. The number "seven" was more often used in our conversations with the younger women, though. Whether or not everyone does this today, we were fortunate to have been invited to celebrate Christmas Eve at the home of someone who had made sure we were served seven different kinds of cookies when it came time for dessert!

Meanwhile, laughter greeted us when we announced that *lutefisk* would be served ceremoniously at the Shiell home for Christmas, as it had been for both Diane and Dell since they were kids! Over and over we were told that not all Norwegians, especially not the younger people, bothered with the ceremonial serving of this jellied mass of fish—not even at Christmastime.

Norwegians were interested in knowing about American Christmas traditions. For example, did we use Christmas trees? "Sure," we answered. They already knew this. We were just being set up for the follow-up question about the common use of artificial Christmas trees in the USA. It was fun to have been able to cite some surprising statistics for our Norwegian friends. Did they know that each year Americans use 34 million "live" Christmas trees, in addition to about the same number of artificial trees? We did not know that until we read it in an American newspaper, while we lived in Larvik. What amazed us was that Christmas trees sold in Norway were most often grown in Denmark. This seemed incredible when we first heard it because pine tree forests were one of the most common sites everywhere we went in Norway. When others saw the puzzled look on our faces, they explained the logic behind this practice. The problem is one of logistics and economics. It simply costs too much to harvest small trees from a rugged mountainside to be sold as Christmas trees. It makes better sense to let those trees grow and use them as lumber and other wood products. The flat land of Denmark is much more suitable for growing and harvesting Norway's Christmas trees—and the Danish trees are cheaper, too.

Of course, if you have the opportunity to cut down your own

Christmas tree and bring it home, then you are going to bring home a Norwegian tree! We happened to have some friends who made it possible for us to do just that. Our Christmas tree saga began in October when we tramped into the woods to pick out our tree before the snow fell. We marked our tree by tying a red ribbon on it. No one else would take that tree. In early December, we returned to cut down and bring our tree to town. Did it go into the house, then? No. We were told that in Norway one doesn't put up the Christmas tree until Christmas. By getting the tree early one didn't have to worry about impassable roads into the mountains at Christmastime. You had your tree sitting in the backyard, ready and waiting for Christmas.

"Caring for everyone" seems to be the theme of the Norwegian Christmas season. Extra grain is given to horses and cows to assure the health of the animals during the coming year. Even the smallest animals are remembered. One tradition is to hang a sheaf of grain on a pole for the birds. The sheaves of grain are the last of the harvest and were set aside for the birds. The sheaves tied to the pole are called *julenek*. According to another tradition, even the mice are to be spared at Christmastime. We were told by a neighbor that during the Christmas season he left his mousetraps in the cellar unset. He had three mice down there, but this was something to be tolerated at Christmas. The day before he said this, a refugee family from Yugoslavia had been told that they must leave Norway. Our neighbor was lamenting on how sad it was that Norwegians would spare the mice but send this refugee family away at Christmastime. Many people in Larvik felt the same as he did and there was considerable public protest. Many of the school children became involved in the protest. One of the children in the Yugoslavian family was a classmate of Ian's. Ian and his class were anxious for their friend and wrote letters to the government on her family's behalf. When the deadline arrived, a parish pastor organized an all-night prayer vigil at the Larvik Church. The Yugoslavian family was present and many wondered if the police would enter the church to remove this family from the sanctuary. The authorities agreed to delay the expulsion and review the case after the first of the year.

All creatures are to be remembered and fed. Even a few characters of legend are remembered. An old custom in rural areas is to put a bowl of *risgrøt* (porridge) in the barn for the *nisse*. The *nisse* is a little elf who resides in the barn all year to take care of everything. You try to keep the *nisse* happy. If you do not, he might cause you to have bad luck all year. If you keep your *nisse* happy you are likely to have the fattest cows and the smartest children in your village.

In the USA, many different cultural traditions are blended together. In Norway, most families have the same traditions and these do not change much over the years. One adopted tradition is the *Julenisse*, the Christmas *Nisse*. They do not have Santa Claus. Santa was so popular in other countries that Norwegians created their own version—the *Julenisse*. He looks similar to Santa. He has a white beard and wears a red suit.

There is a certain sense of security in having things done the same way each year. As the Christmas season begins, the streets become *julegater* (Christmas streets). In many homes there is a seven branched candle holder lit in the window. Today most of these lights are electric, but they are beautiful to behold as you walk down the dark evening streets. A big Christmas tree was put up in the Larvik town square, and it is an annual event which young and old look forward to.

Simple foods became both special and a Christmastime event. We were invited to the homes of friends for rice pudding (*risgrøt*) or rice boiled in milk with sugar on it. An almond was hidden in the pot. The person who found the almond in his bowl would have good luck (or get married before the next Christmas, whichever appeals to the person finding the almond). It is amazing how often that almond turned up in the bowl of one of our children that

Christmas. Ian was the first to find an almond in his *jule-risgrøt*. He was at a Boy Scout Christmas party. The prize he won for finding the almond was a candy marzipan pig. People were gracious and wanted us to experience their traditions.

Diane cleaned the house before Christmas, but she did not wash the walls and ceiling. When you heat with wood, the ceiling does get a little grimy. We were still adjusting to heating with wood. Washing ceilings was an adjustment yet to come. So, we probably failed the cleaning tradition, but we should have passed the baking tradition (at least the seven kinds' version). We introduced friends to homemade carmelcorn. We baked our own traditional Christmas cookies using Grandma's old Scandinavian recipes. Diane baked a *kransekake* (a tiered, ring cake) from scratch, using a recipe from a Norwegian cookbook—a total failure. Diane admitted this failure to someone and the woman replied, "Oh, no, we buy the dough in the grocery store." Sure enough, Diane produced a perfect *kransekake*. A friend later told Diane that she always baked her own *kransekake* and she would show Diane how. The friend was an excellent cook. An evening was set aside and Diane was the student. In the end, the friend's *kransekake* turned out just like Diane's first one had. She was dismayed and Diane was encouraged. If an expert could fail there was hope for Diane and a reason to try again. So, try she did, and soon Diane had several successes making *kransekake* from scratch. The final major Christmas masterpiece from our kitchen was a gingerbread house. Earlier we admired one in someone else's home. We asked if they had a pattern for it. No, they bought theirs at the store. We were dubious, but there they were at the local grocery store, boxes with all the pre-cut pieces of gingerbread. They called them *pepperkakehus*. Four of us kept busy for two hours, putting this house together and decorating it; Dell got in on the finishing touches. We were so proud of our masterpiece. That afternoon we were interviewed by a reporter for the local paper. The resulting article was about

Christmas in the USA. As the photographer was getting ready to take our picture for the article, he noticed our gingerbread creation. He placed it on the table in front of our family and took our photograph. The industrious Americans made a good impression when this picture appeared in the paper.

Decorations in the USA, by Norwegian standards, are gaudy. Norwegian Christmas decorations are much simpler. Few, if any, outside lights were used; if they were used, they were white, not many bright colors. Straw goats of various sizes were abundant. One goat tradition goes back to Viking days when a person would put on a goat skin and goat head and enter a party. During the party the person dressed as the goat would die and come back to life. A typical Norwegian Christmas tree would have on it some small straw goats, strings of small Norwegian flags, mice, white lights resembling candles, and heart baskets made by the children. Our tree ended up having many Shiell decorations on it. Megan and Ian went to a special activity at school to make ornaments and decorations. One Saturday, our family was invited to someone's home to make ornaments. The little heart baskets the children made were to be filled with candy, but this candy was not to be eaten until Christmas.

If Norwegians were to choose the one time they were the most likely to go to a restaurant to eat, it would be at Christmastime. This meal was so special that it had its own title—*julebord*. We heard that these meals were fantastic. The *julebord* is served in a restaurant and set up like a *smorgasbord* in Minnesota. Favorite Norwegian foods were served, as well as speciality foods like reindeer meat and salmon. The *julebord* is an old tradition going back to times when Norwegians left a table spread with food for the spirits of the dead at Christmastime. For our family, the *julebord* would have cost about $150. We skipped the *julebord*.

As Christmas approaches, the house is clean, your seven kinds of cookies are made, your gifts have been purchased and you probably did not go into debt because the gifts are much simpler, more practical and far fewer. Your Christmas tree is in your backyard waiting to be put up on the twenty-third or twenty-fourth. Most likely you have purchased ribs as your main meat for your Christmas meal. The tradition of eating pork ribs goes back to the winter solstice celebrations of the Vikings. Pigs were slaughtered and eaten during a feast to celebrate the fact that the sun was returning. Darkness and cold would leave, and sunlight and warmth would return. (Our tree went up on the twentieth and we purchased two ducks in Denmark for our main meat.) It is almost Christmas and you greet everyone with *"Gledelig Jul"* or *"God Jul."*

At 4:00 on Christmas Eve, the church bells began to ring and could be heard all over town. Church was at 5:00 p.m. Dell had the service at the smaller of the two churches in Larvik. The church was filled to capacity and beyond. Sitting in the pew, along with our family, were Dell's parents—Wendell and Ruth Shiell—who had come to Larvik to celebrate Christmas with us. Many of the Christmas hymns were familiar, but we were surprised at the number of our traditional hymns not known to Norwegians because these hymns came from different cultures. The most popular Christmas hymn was *"Deilig er Jorden"* (Beautiful is the Earth), but the surprise was that it was sung to the tune of "Beautiful Savior." After dinner we opened gifts. Our family tradition is to open gifts on Christmas Eve. The children were taught in school that ALL Americans open their gifts on Christmas Day. A Norwegian tradition is to join hands, walk around the Christmas tree, and sing. Of course this meant the tree was not placed right up to the wall.

We were invited for coffee and cookies at the home of friends late Christmas Eve. They lived only two blocks away and the walk there was like a walk in a fairy land, or at least like a scene from *White Christmas*. It was mild, about 35 degrees, there was no wind and huge snowflakes floated from above. The dim street lamps and the lights in every window gave the evening a Christmas magic. A special Christmas, a special time, a special place.

Christmas Day is called the first day of Christmas and there were worship services. The day after Christmas is called the second day of Christmas and there were worship services. The night before the second day of Christmas Dell was called and asked to fill in for another pastor the next morning. There was always added stress when there was a limited time to prepare for a service.

The next special worship service was on New Year's Eve. Dell led this worship service. A large group of teenagers from *KUF* attended the service which made it especially meaningful for Dell. Diane, Megan, and Ian stayed home and enjoyed watching the Norwegians celebrate the new year. They used fireworks! We were amazed. It looked like our Fourth of July. Diane, Megan, and Ian climbed the *fjell*, or large granite hill, at the end of our street. They looked over the city and saw the colored lights everywhere. The fireworks were set off by individuals in their yards rather than in one central location. Dell timed the service so that the ending bell tolled at midnight. Because of the warm weather many people were in the streets to hear the bells of the new year.

According to Norwegian tradition, we put our Christmas tree up too early, and we took it down too early. We had pine needles covering the floor and a new layer fell every time someone passed the tree or walked too hard on the wood floor. For us, Christmas was over; it was January. Of course it wasn't really over; we were in Norway and Christmas continues for two weeks. Before Christmas, every organization had a Christmas party. After Christmas, they had *juletrefests*—Christmas tree parties. January is a dark month and to avoid the "after Christmas blues" there are parties, many parties, to chase away the dark January days.

We attended three *juletrefests*. The hospital had one for their employees and their families. The elementary school had a *juletrefest* for all the children and their families, and *KUF* had a *juletrefest* for families, young and old. We got better at celebrating as we figured out what was expected of participants. Everyone joins hands and forms two rings around the Christmas tree. Music is played, and the groups walk around the Christmas tree, each ring going in the opposite direction. Everyone sings and many of the songs are children's songs. The favorite song? From what we saw, everyone's favorite was the Norwegian version of "This is the way we wash our clothes, early Monday morning" and the following verses.

At our first parish in Minnesota we were introduced to the *julebukk* custom. Some college students came to our home dressed in costume, wanting treats, and wouldn't speak. We had to guess who they were. *Julebukk* means Christmas goat. Long ago young people in costume went from farm to farm with a goat's head on the end of a stick to scare away evil spirits. In Norway some friends decided to share the fun of *julebukk* with the American family. Two women came to our door, in costume, carrying a tray with wine and wine glasses. They wanted us to guess who they were and they wanted treats. They were very lighthearted and their husbands stood outside in the shadows snickering. We appreciated being included in this tradition.

The Christmas season and the days of parties were past. Like so many times in our lives, we were so busy trying to keep up and then suddenly that time was over. We were thankful to those who shared their traditions with us. We were glad we had a Norwegian Christmas. We felt sad as the bells rang on New Year's Eve knowing that next year, even if it was warm enough to stand in the streets at midnight, we wouldn't be able to hear the bells of the Larvik Church.

CHAPTER 8

OUR BARN IN NORWAY

A "kid" is a baby goat and the "barn" is a reasonable place to find a kid. However, in a foreign country it is possible to mix and combine words and their meanings in fun new ways. In Norway, our children were both our American kids and our Norwegian *barn* (Norwegian for "children").

In so many ways it seemed as if we stepped off the plane and started living a normal life. With three kids, there was no time to sit around and adjust. The children's attitude was not, "Let's learn about our new surroundings," but rather, "Let's do things."

Each child had corresponded with one child from Larvik before we arrived. They were excited to meet their new friends. News of our arrival was known to many. The first day at our new home, our children were greeted at the front door by their penpals and other neighborhood children. Most children did not speak English; one girl carried a note that said, "Hi, my name is Jorunn." What did our children do when other kids came to the door? They went out and played. Language was not a hindrance to fun.

Before we left Cedar Rapids, friends from Gloria Dei gave each of our children a priceless gift—a diary. They began writing in their diaries on the plane to Norway, wrote in them every night before going to bed in Norway, and made their last entry on the plane returning home.

Their days were so full, especially at the beginning, that without their diaries many events of those days would have been lost to them. Ian went to swimming lessons on our first Saturday morning; we had arrived in Larvik on Friday afternoon. Both Megan and Ian began swimming lessons the next Saturday. Bethany went to a Y-SING (a youth choir) practice our first week in Norway, and went on a trip with Y-SING to another town in southern Norway, seven days after we landed. Originally, we said "No" to this trip, but Bethany's new friends wanted her to come along. In the end, we did not have a real reason for her to stay at home, unless you count having to figure out what food she needed to take, what clothes she needed, and what she would sleep on. During our first week, we figured out some basics that would last us for the year. Whenever there was an overnight event and food was needed, everyone brought bread and *påleg* (pronounced "poe-legg", a topping). *Påleg* could be jam, cheese, meat, and for Bethany— peanut butter. At each meal the bread and *påleg* was shared by everyone; afterwards, they were put away and used for the next meal.

Megan immediately became a Norwegian Girl Scout and Ian, a Boy Scout. On our third weekend a Girl Scout trip was planned. The Girl Scouts went on an overnight in the mountains. The father taking the group to the mountains invited Dell to go along with Megan and the Girl Scouts. The night before this outing, we were invited to someone's home for coffee. We started to wonder about this trip when, after coffee, our hosts wanted Dell and Megan to try on ski boots and skis which were needed to get to the campsite. Diane could only smile as she realized what they were getting into.

It turned out that they skied into the woods and slept on six feet of snow, after first building lean-tos made of branches they cut off trees. It rained most of the night. Diane was full of sympathy when Megan and Dell returned. They did not need it. They had a super time, fun stories, and a lasting memory. They felt sorry for Diane because she had missed it all.

Norwegian children seemed to us to be much more independent than American children. Perhaps the independence or freedom of school-age children was possible because Larvik was a small town in a small country; the kids went by bike wherever they wanted to go in Larvik. Before our arrival, arrangements had been made so each of our children had a bicycle to ride. Norwegian children did not have to make arrangements to be driven everywhere—they just went. High school kids rode bicycles wherever they wanted to go, also. They could not get a driver's licence until age 18 and then only after a very expensive, mandatory driver's education course.

After one and a half months, the kids acted as if they had lived in Larvik forever. Ian and Megan explored the neighborhood. During one adventure at a nearby creek, they found salamanders and brought them home. Ian and a friend spent hours outdoors, building a "fort" from scraps of lumber. Whereas Ian would have called their completed structure a "fort" back in the USA, in Norway, he and his friend had built a *hytte* (pronounced "hit-ta", a cabin) for themselves. After school, Ian would come home and announce, "Bye. I'm going to work on my *hytte* with Jørgen." Ian, also, quickly figured out the system for returning bottles for a deposit. If he had time on his hands, he would search the neighborhood for empty bottles, take them to the store and place them into a machine which paid him a return deposit. Across from the bottle return machine, Ian discovered a gambling machine. At first we discouraged him from using this machine, but later we gave in; occasionally we tried it ourselves. A coin which was deposited in the machine went down a slot, returning extra coins if your coin went in the proper slot. These machines were often operated by charities to make money. Everyone knew that the machine came out ahead, but people were much more likely to put a coin in this machine than in a box marked, "Donation."

The children quickly learned how to have fun. Since they wanted to play with other kids, they learned their games. It was nice to see children in the backyard playing a game, laughing, and having fun. A popular game was *lærerball* (teacher's ball). Megan and her friends spent a lot of time playing *hoppestrikk*, a version of Chinese jumprope. Some days when other children were not available, our children actually found a ball and played together! The children often stayed overnight with friends and went to birthday parties.

Invitations to birthday parties began arriving our first month and continued throughout the year. Norwegian children dressed up for these parties. When they attended birthday parties at our home, they were extremely polite as well as dressed up. Before we left Cedar Rapids, Ian had nine boys over for a birthday party and they were totally out of control. In Norway, he had nine boys at his birthday party also, but they were polite, well-behaved and dressed for a special occasion. The contrast was so great! We combined our own menu with a typical Norwegian birthday menu. Typical Norwegian party food was cake, plain jello with vanilla sauce, plain hot dogs (no bun), and plain mashed potatoes (no butter or gravy—nothing). It seemed that a birthday party was the only time mashed potatoes were served. For our parties, we served cake and ice cream, pizza, and plain jello with vanilla sauce. (Once a family invited us for dinner and they were not sure what to serve us. To make sure it was something we would enjoy, they served their traditional birthday meal.) At a birthday party the children sang, "Happy Birthday" or "Happy *Bursdag*." The birthday greeting was, *Gratularer med dagen* (Congratulations with the day).

We thought that most of the Norwegian names would be familiar to us. How wrong we were. Here are some of the names of our children's friends. Boys' names included: *Kjell, Frode, Kjetil, Atle, Øystein, Terje, Wiggo, Vebjørn.* Some of the girls' names were: *Gro, Guro, Aud, Gølin, Tove, Tille, Anika, Eivor, Åse, Inger.* (Something we learned early was that names ending with "e" were pronounced as though they ended with an "a." So, "Diane" was pronounced as "Diana.") It was much easier for our children to remember the unfamiliar sounding names than for us because they did not have preconceived ideas of what a Scandivavian name was.

Two months after we arrived, Bethany went on another trip with Y-SING. This time the group went to Denmark to perform at churches. We were not in the habit of giving our 13-year-old daughter permission to leave the country. It was strange for us to say, "Good-bye. Have fun. Do you have your passport?" It was a great opportunity for Bethany, though. The group gave her a special role in their program. They asked her to read the poem, "Footprints," in English, to the audience. She was scared, but she wanted to do it anyway. We were proud of her, it would have been easy for her to avoid doing this.

Teenage kids did not babysit to earn money. People just did not get someone to watch their children when they went out, but then they did not go out much. It was strange to drive past a restaurant on a Saturday night and see only one or two cars parked outside. The young girls did earn money by walking babies in carriages so the mothers could have a break at home. Carriages were used a lot. One mother said she put her child in the backyard and left him there in his carriage while she did the housework. This was a good way for her child to get plenty of fresh air. Many mothers shared this philosophy and wanted their children to be taken for daily walks outside. Megan walked a baby named Kristofer for several months. Kristofer was very young when Megan started to take him for a walk. We all fell in love with him; it was a horrible experience to leave Norway and to leave Kristofer. Often Diane and Bethany walked with Megan and Kristofer downtown, to look in the shops. They took turns staying outside with Kristofer. They did not practice the Norwegian custom of leaving the baby outside the shop unattended. Megan shared her job with Bethany so that they could both earn a little spending money. Ian earned a little money by bringing fire wood into the house each day. Most of our kids' friends seemed to have plenty of money to spend; our kids had a hard time to keep up with them.

There were often parties for the children to attend at homes and at school. The school parties were organized with games, dancing, and pizza. The adults did not seem to go out frequently, but they organized parties for the children.

Dell mentioned to someone that Ian liked to fish. The church council president and his ten-year-old grandson invited Ian to go fishing with them. What an experience! With three hooks on his line, Ian caught three fish at a time. Before they came back to shore those two boys had caught 52 mackerel. Once ashore, the proud grandfather quickly took a picture of the equally proud boys with their pails full of fish.

One evening a stranger called and asked Dell if he and two of our children would like to go fishing in the Larvik *fjord*. He had heard from a friend that Dell and the children were looking for opportunities to fish. The plans were hastily made and Dell, Megan and Ian were off to meet this man at his boat. They would be home by 10:00 p.m. At 11:00 p.m. Diane was worried—by midnight she was feeling panicky. She had no idea who the man was, or who his friend was for that matter. She only knew that the boat was too small to take Bethany with them and that the Norwegians have a habit of not using life jackets when out on a boat. They returned a little after midnight, proud of the *torsk* (cod) that they caught. Diane was not in the mood for fish stories. She kissed them goodnight and slept soundly, while on the front step, under the light of a 25 watt bulb, until 2:00 a.m., Dell fileted fish with a dull knife.

Bethany joined a dance group. This group competed in a district-wide contest and won the semi-finals. She was so excited. The competition was held at a town about 45 miles from Larvik. Bethany and her friends took the train to the event. For Bethany, taking the train with her friends was half of the fun. To her friends, taking the train was just a means of transportation, not an adventure. After the girls won the semi-finals competition, they went on to the finals. It had been impossible for our family to go to the semi-finals, but it was merely difficult for us to attend the finals. Dell and Ian were gone for the weekend and they had the car. Bethany, Megan, and Diane decided to take the train to the city hosting the finals. At least they took the train to a bus stop; they took a bus the rest of the way to Horton. Again the trip was the adventure, but one that had a story that our Norwegian friends loved to hear.

Diane and the girls had a map of Horton. When they arrived downtown at the end of the bus line, Diane asked the bus driver for directions to the building they were looking for. "Ach," he said. The girls caught enough of his rapid Norwegian to tell Diane that the school was a long walk from where they were. Maps are often deceiving. The bus driver told Diane and the girls to sit down and he started up the empty bus. Diane and the girls had no idea where they were going. By the map they knew they were not going to the school where the competion was. They ended up at the bus garage. The driver told them to get out. He parked the bus and soon backed out his own car. They climbed in and he drove them right up to the school they were looking for. He did not speak any English. Diane tried to supply him with a little information about who they were and why they were in Norway. The girls giggled in the back seat as Diane struggled through one of her longest Norwegian dialogues. The driver understood who they were and at least had enough information to tell his wife about the Americans he had rescued that day. We were always treated very graciously. We're sure many Americans can tell about the hospitality of their Norwegian relatives and friends. Norwegians often talk about the kindnesses shown to them in the USA. What makes our experience with the bus driver unique is that Norwegians told us that they feel that Americans are much more likely to help strangers than Norwegians are likely to help strangers. When we told this tale Norwegians would smile, nod, and breath a sigh of relief as if to say, "Yes, it can happen here, too."

Dell and Ian were on a Boy Scout camping trip that weekend. They stayed at a mountain *hytte* (a log cabin) which belonged to a lumber company. The *hytte* had no plumbing or electricity. At night, indoor lighting was provided by many candles in candleholders on tables and mounted on the walls. The boys hiked in the mountains, studied the night sky, and developed their camping skills.

The children love to swim and they went swimming whenever they could. Megan and Ian took swimming lessons during our entire stay. The Larvik community pool was centrally located. It was across the street from all three schools: elementary, junior high, and high school. The pool was used by the schools during school hours. In the evenings and on weekends, it was used by the community. When you come from Iowa, swimming pools are the number one place to swim. In Norway, people seem to have a bias toward either swimming in the sea or a lake. The children were often asked, "Do you like to swim in salt water or fresh water?" A pool was never an option. This was a loaded question, the children found out, and they learned to be little diplomats. People preferred the body of water that their *hytte* (summer home) was sitting on. Your heart goes the way of your pocketbook. Our children answered the way the questioner wanted them to because they really enjoyed both. They did find a favorite swimming place in Larvik. Coming up to the city is a seven-mile-long lake. A friend had a summer home near it and access to the perfect swimming spot. The water was clear (and cold) and the lake bottom where we swam was solid rock. A little way from shore, a large rock rose up out of the water; it was sun-soaked and warm. After a short swim in the icy water it offered a reward of warmth and rest.

Bethany's schoolmates were a year older than she so they were confirmed soon after we arrived in Larvik. Dell and Bethany planned to study together so that Bethany could be confirmed with her class at Gloria Dei after we returned home. We brought her study materials along to Norway. Bethany's confirmation studies turned out to be fun for her. Just as school was ending, Dell was approached by a woman whose daughter wanted to be confirmed in the Church of Norway. The daughter lived at a boarding school in Scotland. This meant that Gry, the daughter, could not prepare for confirmation with other Norwegian youth. Gry's father worked for Shell Oil and the family lived abroad a lot. Like her older brother, Gry was to receive stability and a good education while attending this Scottish school. At school she was instructed in the Presbyterian faith and attended chapel daily, as was expected of all the students. Bethany's confirmation materials were very useful. Dell used sections of these materials and gave Gry assignments to do in English, something she was quite used to doing. Bethany and Gry met with Dell throughout the summer, as Bethany continued her confirmation studies and Gry completed her instruction. Bethany enjoyed having someone to study with and became friends with Gry. Gry was confirmed at Langestrand Church before returning to school in Scotland in the fall.

The end of the 1989 school year in Norway for our children was not the end of the school year for everyone else. We left in March. Usually Bethany's class took a class trip at the end of the year and had a class picture taken at the end of the year. At parent conference time, in February, Bethany's homeroom teacher told us that Bethany's class had asked her to have it arranged so that both the class trip and class picture could take place before Bethany left. Bethany and her class took their trip to Oslo where they went to a theater performance. Bethany also has a picture of her Norwegian class and she is in it. Bethany's classmates also asked her to give a speech about Cedar Rapids before she left Larvik. Before we left the USA, a friend at the Cedar Rapids Chamber of Commerce had supplied us with some excellent materials which both Megan and Bethany used for class reports. After Bethany gave her report, a couple of girls checked into the possibility of becoming foreign exchange students. On another occasion, Bethany gave a report on what it is like to be a teenager in the USA compared to being a teenager in Norway.

Not all our goals and dreams come true. Sometimes they do and we have been blessed. When our children were very young, we had a dream. This dream took into consideration that adolescence is a difficult time in a child's life. Peers, conformity, and the willingness to accept blindly the values of your friends are often very important parts of an adolescent's life. Our dream wasn't to cause our children culture shock; we just wanted them to see that there is a world beyond their small group. Our year in Norway did not radically change our kids, but we hadn't wanted that. That year did help our kids to see that things do not have to be done only one way; often there is another way, a different way.

When we saw the friendships our children made, we were thankful for the timing of this exchange in our lives. Before we left Cedar Rapids, we said jokingly that we had to hurry up and get our children to another country before they were old enough to want to marry. We felt that our children were old enough to appreciate the experience, but young enough so that they would not fall in love, get married, and end up living in Norway. We had thought that we were only putting our family in another country for one year and then pulling them out again. We realize now that the experience didn't end when we left Norway; letters and visits from Norwegian friends are an ongoing part of our lives. In the summer of 1990, Bethany and Megan made their first return trip to Norway to visit friends for a month.

Before we left Cedar Rapids, the children were proud of the new clothes they had purchased to take to Norway. They had "Coke" sweatshirts and sweaters, "Reebok" tennis shoes, and "Guess" jeans. They were in for a surprise; their friends in Larvik had not heard of any of these brands when we arrived. The kids decided that they could be wearing "generic" clothes instead. They still liked their clothes, but it was not the same as when your friends could identify the brand name. They had learned something, right? Well, maybe. "BALL" was the popular brand name in Norway and Denmark. Ian saved his money and bought a $50 BALL sweatshirt. Again, he was so proud of it. He wore it to school often. When we got back to Cedar Rapids Ian wore it twice and then left it in his drawer. He was willing to wear it for a family outing, but not to school. For Bethany's birthday, we gave her a beautiful leather backpack for school; one like all the other kids had. She was so proud of it, but back in Cedar Rapids it went into a closet and was not used. Maybe our children learned something, maybe they did not. Maybe we, as parents did. Peers are important. The kids were willing to adjust in both countries, they only wanted to fit in. In their defense, they did go the whole year with very few new clothes. Clothing was expensive and purchases were saved for special occasions. Ian's favorite jeans were getting a hole in the knee, so the last month in Norway he did not wear them to school. He wanted to save them for the plane ride home, hoping that they were still in style back home.

We arrived home late on a Sunday evening. After the long flight, we had a five-hour drive from Chicago to Cedar Rapids. The children were back in school in Cedar Rapids on Tuesday. Soon after we returned home Megan had a writing assignment for her

sixth grade language arts class. She wrote this poem:
> The tears and laughs
> are mixed up inside.
> All because
> of an airplane ride.

CHAPTER 9

WAS THAT LUTEFISK AND LEFSE — OR WAS IT HOT DOGS AND LEFSE?

When we first arrived we had trouble figuring out when to eat. Norwegian meal times were different than ours. Again, this is changing because more women are working outside the home, but most people in Larvik still ate at the traditional Norwegian meal times. Breakfast was eaten before school or work. Lunch was a sandwich at your desk—work or school—around noon. We were in sync there. Dinner was eaten in the late afternoon, around 3:00 p.m. or 4:00 p.m. Meetings for Dell were often scheduled at 5:00 p.m. or 6:00 p.m. We tried adjusting to the Norwegian meal times and ate around 4:00 p.m. We weren't very hungry, and the worst result was that everyone was hungry again around 8:00 p.m. or 9:00 p.m. That is when the Norwegians eat their fourth meal (a big snack). Diane did not think fixing four meals a day for a year

97

sounded too great. We ended up eating as close to our customary meal times as we could. We adjusted our schedules each day and tried to eat together sometime between 4:30 p.m. and 6:30 p.m. This worked as long as we were eating as a family. If we were entertaining or going to someone's home we had to rethink our meal times. We realized this after two mistakes. Yes, it took two. The first time we were invited to someone's home in the afternoon on a Sunday. We ate a substantial dinner at home at 1:00 p.m. We forgot that their main meal is around 3:00 p.m. At 3:00 p.m. they brought out a large dinner. It was delicious, but we were stuffed. We ate, of course, but we all felt miserable afterward. Another time, we invited a family over for our evening meal on a weekday. They already had eaten their main meal at 4:00 p.m. at home. Both times the Norwegians and we knew food would be served, but neither time had we expected a full meal. The mistake was on our part and we learned to eat at their times when it involved other people.

We weren't accustomed to eating out very often in the USA, but we hadn't realized that once in Norway we wouldn't have fast food restaurants to help us out in a pinch. In Larvik, there were no McDonalds, Pizza Hut, or Chinese take-out. We had a family of five who wanted to eat three meals every day. Diane suggested that maybe it would be fun to skip dinner once in awhile, but she never had any takers. The family always wanted to eat. Twice that year we succumbed to our only take-out option. The local grocery store had small prepared whole chickens. We'd buy two, fix a salad, and Mom had the night off. The problem was that the chickens were $8.00 apiece.

For breakfast we ate granola, toast, and orange juice. We found a brand of granola we loved and indulged ourselves. It was $5.00 a box. Before we left Cedar Rapids, a friend jokingly said she would have to send us some Captain Crunch. The grocery store did not have a full aisle of breakfast cereal as we do, but they did have Captain Crunch, called *Skipper Spør* with the same captain, and Frosted Flakes with Tony the Tiger. It was fun to see familiar faces. The kids traded breakfast traditions with their friends. When friends stayed at our home they liked having cereal for breakfast.

A typical Norwegian breakfast is bread with *påleg* (a generic word for a topping), usually marmalade or cheese. Bethany learned to prefer a Norwegian breakfast. One cereal that was popular was called *museli*. It was not sold in packages like the cereal companies offer it in the USA. *Museli* as we often saw it was a large bowl of cornflakes and a large bowl of uncooked oatmeal. You simply put them together in a cereal bowl and put milk on it. Orange juice was purchased in one-liter unrefrigerated containers. The containers were similar to the small individual drink boxes that we are familiar with. A can of frozen orange juice concentrate was a luxury.

We learned another variation of *museli* from one of Ian's friends whose father was from Switzerland. We adapted the recipe and it is still a favorite breakfast today.

Museli

Melt 2 tablespoons butter in a frying pan.
Add 4 cups rolled oats (not quick oats).
Add 1 cup chopped or sliced nuts
      (we always use almonds — they were readily
      available in Norway, and remain our favorite).
Lightly brown the oats and nuts over low heat, stirring
      frequently.
Sprinkle 1 tablespoon sugar on top of oats and nuts.
After this mixture cools, store it in an airtight
      container.
Mix 1 part plain yogurt and 1 part fruit yogurt.

We put the yogurt and the oatmeal mixture on the table. Proportions are up to the individual. Each person takes yogurt and adds the oatmeal-nut mixture.

One of the children and Diane went grocery shopping about three times a week. Milk was sold in one-liter cartons. That is like buying all your milk in one-quart cartons. We always needed milk and because we were walking we could carry home only about four bags each. We never saw a paper sack in Norway. All the bags were plastic. They were a heavy plastic, great for carrying groceries home, but we were concerned about the number of plastic sacks we accumulated. We've read, since returning home, that those bags were biodegradable, but... We learned to conserve on trash. We were allowed only one large trash bag per week. It can be done when you have to.

Coffee was sold only in packages, equivalent to one pound. The Norwegian formula for making coffee explains why grocery carts were loaded with one pound bags of coffee when coffee was on sale. We drink a lot of coffee, but we had to learn to drink Norwegian coffee. Here is the formula: one scoop (like a scoop that comes with a coffeemaker) for each cup of coffee you are making and then "one extra scoop for the pot." So, an eight-cup coffeemaker takes nine scoops. We expressed incredulity our first week and word got around. For our first two months our hosts always had a pot of boiling water ready to "cut" our coffee. That was extremely considerate, but we learned to drink the strong Norwegian coffee. We also learned where people got the idea that a spoon might be able to stand up in a cup of coffee.

Believe it or not, trips to the grocery stores were educational. At the store everything was sold in liters, grams and kilograms. Prices were advertised this way, you had to weigh produce on a metric scale, and ask for meat and cheese in kilograms. The children used only the metric system in school. This was difficult, but we were able to help the children incorporate it into our daily life. Not only did the metric system come in handy at the grocery store, but each morning one of the kids checked the temperature outside and converted the temperature from Celsius to Fahrenheit.

We had to learn new names for so many items in the store. It was not enough to know the Norwegian word for "flour." We had to know the names for different kinds of flour—wheat, rye, cracked wheat, white. Oatmeal and other kinds of cereal grains came in what looked to us like flour packages, too. Spices were also complicated. When we returned home we found that the Norwegians had written the Norwegian name on many of the spice containers in our cupboard. Over time we figured things out. We must have looked confident—not like Americans who didn't know what they were doing—because we were often stopped in the store and asked if we knew where an item was located.

Shopping was a cultural experience. We all became excited when we saw jars of *torsk* (cod) baby food. That discovery told us we were in Norway, not Iowa. Whole fish—head, tail, and all— were sold in the frozen food section. We adjusted to the frozen fish and then had another surprise. One day we saw a frozen bird in the frozen food section; a whole bird, with all its white feathers on. We were told it was a special bird called *rippa* found above the tree line in the mountains.

There were foods we did not enjoy, but not so many. We did not enjoy fish pudding and fish balls. We avoided eating a black sausage when it was served because we had read the label and found out it was horse sausage. Their ketchup and mustard were much too sweet for us. We did not enjoy *gammelost* (old cheese). Only Dell liked *geitost* (the brown goat cheese). *Lapskaus* was a common kind of stew or hash. *Kjøttkaker* were meat cakes served with fried onions. Homemade *lapskaus* and *kjøttkaker* were good, but we didn't care for the canned forms that were widely used. We were amazed by the number of prepackaged foods commonly used.

People ate a lot of mutton, not lamb. We were guests at someone's home, the meal was late and the children were starving. The food was put out and the children were told to go first. Ian embarrassed us by taking a large piece of meat. He sat next to a little boy and the boy said to Ian, "Oh, you like sheep." Next followed the exercise of trying to get the meat from Ian's plate to Dell's plate without being too obvious.

We learned to love *Norvegia* cheese, *Jarlsberg* cheese, *Freia* chocolate candy bars, and salt and pepper potato chips. The children learned to like a Norwegian sandwich spread called *Nuggati*. It is like chocolate frosting you eat on bread.

We also ate a lot of *torsk* and herring—pickled herring. People had trouble believing that Diane had grown up eating herring. We were also familiar with *torsk* which made it a favorite meal. *Torsk* was sold also at a reasonable price; it cost only about the same as it would in Iowa. People often boiled their fish, but we tried it that way only once. Going to the fish market was an experience. We bought fish we were familiar with, or we told the clerk we wanted something that tasted like *torsk*. On days we felt daring, we pointed and tried something new. We didn't write down names of fish, so we still don't know what we ate.

And what was our favorite food? Pizza, of course. Pizza is fast becoming popular in Norway. However, we couldn't get pepperoni pizza. In the large tourist cities we could, but in the smaller towns pepperoni was unavailable. We were told, "Sure, you can get pepperoni pizza." But, we suffered a communication gap; people thought we meant paprika pizza—pizza with red peppers. We did not eat pizza at the local pizza restaurant; its cost was greater than our desire for restaurant pizza. We did eat pizza almost weekly though; Diane made it entirely from scratch. The dough was made and spread out. The sauce was homemade, the cheese was shredded and the pepperoni was cut in thin slices. Yes, we had pepperoni. No one knew what we were talking about so we went shopping for it—in Denmark.

We found a satisfactory pepperoni-like sausage in Denmark. We had to pick the whole peppers out of it, but that was a small price to pay. It might sound extravagant to say we went to Denmark for our pepperoni, (a six-and-one-half hour boat ride from Larvik), but in fact we did much of our grocery shopping in Denmark. For many items, the price in Denmark was only twice the price we were used to paying in Iowa. That was an exciting revelation. We bought most of our hamburger in Denmark. We bought small chickens and Danish sausage. Sometimes we were lucky and got a couple of heads of iceberg lettuce. We could rarely find it in Norway; when we did the price was out of sight, but we would pay it. A tossed salad in Norway was made with chinese cabbage (celery cabbage), pineapple, apple, cucumber, green pepper, red pepper, tomato and 1000 island dressing without the "islands."

Norwegians often ate fish, rice, boiled potatoes, and bread. If you ask a Norwegian staying in the USA what food she misses most from Norway she will probably say, "Oh, the bread." We were used to eating wheat and cracked wheat bread back home, but we enjoyed fresh baked Norwegian bread, too. The bread is excellent and they are proud of it. It was fun going to the small neighborhood bakeries to buy it. One of the kids usually volunteered to get the bread and enjoyed a pastry as their reward.

A popular Norwegian sweet bun is called *boller*. We had to learn to like *boller*—they are much heavier than most sweet rolls we eat. Diane also had to learn to make these buns. Bethany came home from school one day and said she had to bring two dozen *boller* for a bake sale at school. We would have been a little more confident making chocolate chip cookies—except they did not sell chocolate chips. We accepted this baking challenge and got a friend of Bethany's to translate a *boller* recipe. This recipe was translated for us and the conversions below are fairly close. The buns turned out the first time we made them and Bethany had two dozen *boller* for her bake sale. The need for *boller* came up a few times during the year, and Bethany's *boller* were always a little different from those brought by her friends. Norwegians used cardamom in most baked goods and we grew tired of this spice, so Bethany's *boller* were the ones with half cardamom and half cinnamon.

Boller

8-9 cups flour
1 cup sugar
1 teaspoon salt
2 teaspoons cardamom;
or 1 tsp. cardamom and 1 tsp. cinnamon
1 package yeast
1 cup melted butter
4 cups scalded milk, cooled to lukewarm
Raise the dough until double
Make into buns (a little smaller than hamburger buns)
Raise the buns for 20 minutes
On a greased pan, bake 375 degrees for 10-15 minutes

Baking was a necessity and we baked often. A hindrance was that we had trouble finding baking soda. Baking soda was not used much; usually baking powder was used. When we finally found it, a one ounce package of baking soda cost over a dollar. Baking soda went on the wish list we sent to people who planned to visit us from the USA.

We ate a lot of waffles. It was a big disappointment to one woman when she found out we were familiar with waffles. She thought that they were uniquely Norwegian. We were not used to eating them as the Norwegians did though, we assured her. Their waffle makers make the waffles in a heart shape. After making waffles, they cool them. A good waffle is cold and a little underdone so it is rather soggy. Butter is then spread on them and they are eaten with coffee. They were pretty good, but an alternate version was delicious. A plate of cold waffles was passed around. We spread sour cream on the waffle and then topped it with strawberry jam. Yum.

We were proud whenever we could tell Norwegians that we recognized a unique Norwegian food which we ate back in the USA. *Lutefisk* was always a subject for discussion. We grew up eating it on holidays. Another holiday treat back home was *lefse*. Once we were in a Norwegian family's home and they set a plate of *lefse* on the table. We beamed, "*Ja*, we eat *lefse*, too." "*Nei*," they informed us. "This isn't *lefse*. It's *lompa*; you wrap it around your hot dog. *Lefse* is thicker, square-shaped, dry, and hard. You put moist cloths around it to soften it, then butter and white sugar go on it." We had trouble believing this one. We knew what *lefse* was. So, from then on we bought *lompa* and put butter and sugar on it and called it *lefse*. We also learned to wrap it around hot dogs for a real Norwegian fast food.

The meals we had in people's homes were always excellent. People worked to give us their best and we appreciated the wonderful meals and hospitality. When we were invited for coffee we sat around the large coffee table. A tablecloth was spread, fresh flowers were in the center of the table (it was an accepted practice to bring your hosts fresh flowers), and the candles were lit. Usually two single layer, round cakes covered with whip cream or marzipan were served. Everyone cut a piece of cake as it was passed around. We had to have that explained to us. We stared at that whole cake the first time it was passed to us, trying to figure out what was expected of us. *Smørbrod* and coffee were served, also. Fruit and soda were often served afterward. A favorite soda was *Farris*, a mineral water from Larvik. This natural mineral water was from the only mineral water spring in Norway. The coffeetime was so simple, yet elegant.

The open-face sandwiches (*smørbrød*), which we were served, sometimes were works of art. We went with a couple on a picnic to a park in Oslo. We were still discovering Norwegian specialties, and they brought some of their best to share with us. The open-face sandwiches were lox or salmon, topped with cold scrambled eggs. They were special and very good. We could tell by the looks on the kids' faces that they were not going to eat these sandwiches. Their looks said, "Mom, we won't say anything, and you get us out of this." They were rescued by our gracious hosts. They insisted on giving the children money and sent them to the hot dog stand in the park.

At mealtime we were often told, "You Americans eat like birds." We did eat much less than our friends usually ate. We ate less, but we exercised less, too. We rarely saw an excessively overweight person. People also commented at mealtime about how we held our knife and fork. Before we left Iowa, a Norwegian visitor had dinner in our home. The children were fascinated by the way he used his silverware. Once in Norway, they found themselves being watched by others, and we realized how awkward our way of eating looked to a Norwegian. The Norwegian continued eating with fork in one hand and knife in the other; we were constantly changing our fork from our right hand to the left and back to the right again.

We almost forgot to celebrate Thanksgiving (this is not a Norwegian holiday). Traditions were important to our children, so we planned a mini-feast. Diane's brother and sister-in-law had sent Halloween decorations to the children (Halloween is another American celebration), and the decorations took a slow boat, arriving on November 15. The expandable pumpkins made out of tissue paper were just what we needed to make our home festive on Thanksgiving. The pumpkin decorations were interesting to friends, not because they did not celebrate Thanksgiving, but because pumpkins were not common in Norway. A woman in the

Larvik community had worked for many years in domestic service in New York. She had learned to like pumpkin pie and brought two cans of pumpkin back to Larvik with her after a recent trip to New York. Because she knew our traditions she called us and said she had a gift for us. Just before Thanksgiving she gave us one of her cans of pumpkin. Because of her kindness we had a pumpkin pie for Thanksgiving. We did not have a turkey. Turkeys were available, but we chose not to buy one. A 12-pound turkey would have cost $50. We were not that hungry for turkey. We squeezed our meal into a normal busy day. The children returned home from school at 2:30 p.m. and Dell had a 5:00 p.m. meeting. We had Thanksgiving from 3:30 p.m. to 4:30 p.m. We feasted on two small chickens from Denmark, *tyttebar* (small, wild, mountain cranberries or lingonberries that are very popular in Norway) and a pumpkin pie.

A favorite Norwegian drink is *akevitt* (aquavit), a potent liquor made from potatoes and flavored with caraway seeds. We never got a chance to try it.

One afternoon our family was invited to the home of neighbors for an American barbeque. We had hamburgers on the grill, potato salad, soda pop, potato chips, and brownies. We gulped when we saw all the quarter pounders to be grilled. Each of us had a family of five people and we knew the price of hamburger. We really appreciated that meal. We learned why they were familiar with the ingredients for an American picnic. One of our hosts, like so many others we met in Norway, had been a high school exchange student to the USA. We found out that she had been at a school in the Minneapolis area. She was a senior at a neighboring school in the same athletic conference as Diane's high school when Diane was a high school senior. Even more incredible, they had been to the same football games, sitting on opposite sides of the football field, twenty years before we sat eating our hamburgers in her backyard. It is a small world after all.

CHAPTER 10

AN AMERICAN PRIEST IN NORWAY

The average ratio of Norwegian pastors to church members is one Norwegian pastor for every 4,000 members. In Larvik, the ratio is slightly better, with three pastors for 8,000 members. Before we left the USA, the idea crossed our minds that the Church of Norway decided to take a chance on Dell because they figured that if he were completely useless to them, the Larvik parish would still be only as bad off as the average parish in Norway. Dell made his own contribution as a pastor. He spoke and preached on 130 occasions. He conducted pre-baptismal and pre-funeral visits with 38 families. We should like to believe that by the end of our stay, Larvik was still a little better off than the average parish in Norway.

While in Larvik, Dell served on a church staff as an assistant pastor. Everyone on the staff was very friendly and helpful. No one expected Dell to do everything that Pastor Isaksen did. Still, the staff always made Dell feel like a vital member of their ministry team.

The Larvik Church staff included three pastors (including Dell), one deacon, two organists, one secretary, one *kirketjener* (custodian) and one *klokker* (lay reader). The staff worked well together as they served the two churches in the parish, *Larvik Kirke* and *Langestrand Kirke*.

The senior pastor, Jo Bolstad, had studied in the USA for one year about 35 years earlier. In Larvik, Pastor Bolstad was responsible for administrative leadership of the church staff. Otherwise, all three pastors shared equally in pastoral responsibilities. In addition to parish administration duties, as the senior pastor at the Larvik Church, Pastor Bolstad was automatically the dean for the surrounding conference of parishes.

The resident chaplain (whom we refer to as an assistant pastor) was Eyolf Berg. Both Pastor Bolstad and Pastor Berg spoke English fluently. While they always encouraged Dell to continue to develop his Norwegian language skills, they permitted him to converse with them in English. Of course, this helped Dell immensely.

In Norway, the pastor is called a "priest," and surprisingly that nomenclature is a rather apt description of a Norwegian pastor's duties.

What is the difference between a pastor and a priest? The metaphors associated with each are different. The image associated with a pastor is a shepherd, one who is responsible for the well-being and safety of a small flock. The image associated with a priest, on the other hand, is an official who presides over religious ceremonies. The American pastor is expected to provide pastoral care. The Norwegian priest is expected to officiate at the many religious services required by the realities of a state church. A priest's time is devoted to priestly tasks of worship and its preparations—and that is about all Norwegian clergy have time for.

The Larvik parish provided Sunday worship at 11:00 a.m. in

two church buildings, plus periodic Sunday morning services at *KUF Huset*. Even though so few people attended Sunday morning worship, the pastor had to do the same work as if the church were filled. Each Sunday, Holy Communion was celebrated at one of the two churches and Holy Baptism at the other, with the two sacraments offered alternating weeks at both churches.

We complain about the low church attendance in Norway and the workload of Norwegian pastors. Now, out of the other side of the mouth, we should like to offer the suggestion that the Church of Norway schedule two Sunday morning worship services. We think the option of an earlier service time would attract more people rather than divide the existing few.

Each pastor preached an equal number of Sundays throughout the year. Dell preached at 33 Sunday services. The pastor who preached also served as the liturgist, a practice not at all common for multiple staff situations in the USA! This practice and a rotating preaching schedule for the two churches and *KUF Huset* made it possible for a pastor to have one Sunday a month "off." Perhaps it was not this way throughout Norway, but it was the case in Larvik. It was too good to be true. It was so liberating to be able to plan a family outing once a month. Pastors' families even went to visit relatives on the weekend. That does not mean we skipped church, but we were free to go to another church or to another town, and free to worship as a family.

In Larvik, each pastor took the funerals for a given week. Families could not request a particular pastor for a funeral; they got the pastor "on call," as it were. Dell did not have any funerals the first couple of months. He was busy getting familiar with all his other job responsibilities and learning the language. During our first two months, Pastor Bolstad and Pastor Berg shared Dell's funeral assignments between them.

Of all aspects of the exchange, when we first arrived in Larvik, Dell most feared funerals and pre-funeral family visits. He felt very sensitive to the possibility of failing in this aspect of ministry, given his lack of familiarity with the language. However, once we were settled in, Dell learned to relax and to take even these responsibilities in stride. Afterwards, he said this was a very clear example of God ministering to him so that he might minister to others.

During the remaining months, when Dell was scheduled to take his turn with all the funerals for a given week, he got "lucky." Dell had only 15 funerals. But, those 15 funerals did not represent what was typical for pastors in Norway. For some reason, more people died the weeks when the other two pastors were scheduled to take all the funerals. There were three weeks when Dell was scheduled to have funerals and he did not have a single one! That is very rare. One wonders, "Did people figure out when the American priest was responsible for funerals and purposely choose not to die?" Larvik had an average of three funerals a week or about 150 funerals a year.

In Cedar Rapids, Iowa, at a church with a baptized membership of 550, during the exchange, the Norwegian pastor did not have a single funeral! This was most unusual, since the average number of funerals at this young congregation was three funerals a year. Dell's 15 funerals were significantly below the average in Larvik of around 50 funerals a year per pastor! This is one example of the differences in the availability of time that pastors in each country can devote to pastoral care. This is significant. One might easily wonder whether or not worship attendance in the USA would be any higher than it is in Norway, if American pastors had as little time as Norwegian pastors have to interact with their church members and to help develop church programs of service, witness, fellowship, and Christian education! You cannot put in a 65-hour week in the pulpit and another 40-hour week as church administrator, parish educator, volunteer coordinator, and mission director! There was not nearly the time in Norway for Dell to do the kind of daily ministry he was used to with our congregation in Iowa.

Being a Norwegian church organist was a fulltime job and, like pastors, organists were kept busy. They played for all worship services, funerals, weddings, and all the devotional services at municipal institutions for the sick and elderly. Each week, there were several funerals. A pastor in a neighboring parish told us about an incident involving their organist. One day he had three funerals in a row. After the second funeral, the organist disappeared.

After waiting and searching, the pastor called the organist's home. To his surprise, the organist answered. The pastor told him that everyone was waiting for him to play for the funeral. "Oh," was his response, "Didn't I already play for that one?"

Besides doing a lot of funerals, a Norwegian pastor typically does a lot of baptisms and weddings. Because Dell was not ordained by the Church of Norway, he was not allowed to officiate for any weddings.

Dell did have 23 baptisms. Of course, these were during the regular Sunday morning service at church. Still, this takes quite a lot of a pastor's time. Pastors are not supposed to conduct a baptism without first having a visit with the parents. One Sunday, Dell had five baptisms. That record was broken on another Sunday when he had seven baptisms—four during the service and three afterwards. These were not all members of one or two families, either. Each baptism was a member of a different family unit.

The Larvik pastors shared responsibilities for regular devotional services at six local institutions. These services are called *andakts* and were conducted on a weekly basis. Dell gave 60 *andakts*; of these, 40 were given in an institutional setting. The most frequent institutional setting was the nursing home for the elderly. In Larvik, the pastors took turns "holding an *andakt*" (the expression for these worship services) at four nursing homes for the elderly, one extended-care psychiatric treatment facility, and the municipal hospital. The service usually lasted about one-half hour and was offered once a week in each of these facilities. The only exception was one of the nursing homes which was both a limited care facility and a senior citizen center; here, services were offered once a month.

The order of service for Dell's institutional *andakts* was fairly consistent from week to week. There was an invocation, hymn, scripture reading, homily, hymn, prayer, Lord's Prayer, benediction, and postlude. A church organist was always present to accompany the hymn singing and to play the postlude. Also, as part of the postlude, Dell regularly sang a hymn in English from the *Lutheran Book of Worship* of our church back in the USA.

Usually these *andakts* were conducted in a group setting. However, the hospital *andakt* was announced over the hospital's sound system or intercom. When Dell went to the hospital to hold an *andakt*, he and the organist were alone in a room with a piano and a microphone. Dell would hold his *andakt*, reading, preaching, singing, and praying by himself into the microphone. One week at a staff meeting, the other pastors told Dell that there was a chance that the sound system was not even coming through into the hospital rooms. While this was a source of frustration for the other pastors, it helped to take away some of Dell's anxiety about doing those devotional services.

In addition to these institutional *andakts*, Dell spoke to many different groups and organizations (including the Larvik Rotary Club). Sometimes he was asked to tell something about American church life and to "hold an *andakt*" afterwards. At other times, he was asked to "hold an *andakt*" as part of the agenda during the group's regular meeting. Some such meetings were social gatherings like the senior citizen gathering called an *eldre treff*. It was just as common to be asked to "hold an *andakt*," much like a ten-minute devotional, at the beginning or the end of a regular meeting of various Christian groups. These meetings gave Dell the opportunity to come into contact with a lot of different people in the community. He even recorded five *andakts* that were broadcasted by the local radio station.

The telephone frequently rang with yet another request to "come and hold an *andakt* for us." These requests and the opportunities to bring a devotional message in so many different religious settings in the community were novel experiences for Dell. They taught him that a pastor in the Church of Norway really is a preacher to more than those who attend Sunday worship.

We also became better acquainted with the community in the process. Dell gave an *andakt* in a neighboring parish that celebrated the 800th anniversary of their church, the *Tanum Kirke*. Dell was told an interesting story from the Second World War. Some American fliers were rescued by the Norwegian resistance group in the area. To hide from the Nazis, these Americans were secretly kept in the Tanum Church's belltower, April 22-23, 1945. On Sunday morning, these Americans participated in the parish's worship, without the knowledge of the rest of the congregation. After the Americans had been spirited away to Sweden, the Norwegians found a rosary left behind in the belltower by one of the soldiers who wanted to show his thankfulness to the Norwegians and his trust in God.

The two assistant pastors in Larvik were each assigned two public schools. They visited these schools and organized worship services for the school youth a couple of times a year. Dell was always made to feel welcome in the teachers' lounge of the school, whether elementary, junior high, or high school. He was welcome in the classroom, as well, where he would talk about Christianity or about the church in the USA.

There were around 70 in the confirmation class of the Larvik parish. Dell taught two weekly classes for over half of these confirmation students. Throughout Norway, only one year of confirmation instruction was required, though religious instruction was a required subject every year of school. This school class on Christianity and confirmation instruction provided the chief means of religious education in Norway. Sunday School is virtually non-existent there.

Each pastor determined the curriculum he was going to use for confirmation. When we arrived, Dell was asked which curriculum he planned to use. He attended a workshop on confirmation curriculum and then began to put together his very own confirmation program.

A highlight of the confirmation program was a weekend retreat at a Bible Camp on Oksøya, an island a few miles south of Larvik. Sixty-three confirmation students, fourteen older youth who served as counselors, two pastors, and two cooks traveled by ferry to this island. That ferry was the only transportation back to mainland and it made its stop at this island only by a prearranged appointment. Before they headed out to the island, Dell inquired about ground rules for the retreat, "What about smoking?" He was told smoking was forbidden indoors—otherwise, it was allowed. It was different to play volleyball with 14-year-olds on a confirmation outing and allow them to take a smoke break between games.

Back in Larvik, the matter of confirmation students smoking

presented a practical dilemma. This behavior was tolerated but, as a result of cigarette burns, some carpet was damaged at *KUF Huset* where Dell taught his confirmation classes. Dell suggested that instead of merely restricting smoking to outdoors (as was the rule), youth should be prohibited from smoking on the property. Some adults agreed in principle, but did not want to alienate the kids, so nothing more than a lecture was proposed as the way to prevent future damage.

During Advent, a special worship service was held for the confirmation students and their parents. The service was called a *Lysmesse* (Service of Light). Attendance at this candlelight service, like attendance at the retreat, was mandatory. But the kids seemed eager to participate in both this service and the retreat.

Years ago, the Larvik Church acquired an original oil painting, "Let the little children come unto me" by Lucas Cranach, a contemporary of Martin Luther. Dell learned that one of the more curious "pastoral responsibilities" associated with the Larvik Church was to respond to the request from the local tourist information office to unlock the church to admit tourists into the church to see Cranach's painting.

Another pastoral duty was to be available to parishioners during regular office hours. The church office was open from 10:00 a.m. to 12:00 noon, Tuesday, Wednesday, and Thursday mornings and from 5:00 p.m. to 7:00 p.m. on Friday evening. The three pastors and the deacon split up these office hours, so that each was at the office at least two hours a week.

As a pastor, Dell worked in cooperation with the local chapters of two Norwegian Christian organizations—*KUF* and *Indremisjonen* (in-dre-mish-own-en). *KUF, Kristlelige Ungdomsforening* (The Christian Young People's Association) was the Norwegian YMCA/YWCA. *Indremisjonen* (The Home Mission Society) was an evangelistic organization dedicated to missionary work in Norway, as distinct from foreign missions.

Both *KUF* and The Home Mission Society had their own organizational structures and their own buildings. Larvik *KUF*'s building was called *KUF Huset* (The *KUF* House) and The Home Mission Society's building was called *Bedehuset* (The Prayer

House).

KUF Huset was a fairly new building, located in a residential neighborhood about one mile from the Larvik Church. *KUF Huset*'s building design was very attractive and functional. There was an office, two fellowship dining rooms, several classrooms, a kitchen, basement, and a large, multipurpose meeting room used for worship services and for programs that required use of a stage.

The Home Mission Society had its own building, *Bedehuset*, located closer to the Larvik Church and downtown Larvik. This building was much older than *KUF Huset* and resembled a small, white, wooden, frame church in rural USA. It had one large meeting room with a stage. Instead of pews, however, the room was filled with tables and chairs, indicating a fellowship setting.

Though both Larvik *KUF* and The Home Mission Society of Larvik were independent organizations, both thought of themselves as "arms of the Larvik parish." Both were very "friendly" toward the Larvik parish, and did not see their activity as in competition with the local church.

In fact, numerous fellowship events at both *KUF Huset* and *Bedehuset* served to fill a void in parish life because of inadequate space at the Larvik and Langestrand Churches. Most of what is regarded in the USA as "typical" church activity (with the exception of weekly Sunday morning worship) actually took place at *KUF Huset* and *Bedehuset*.

Larvik *KUF* had a larger membership than the Larvik Home Mission Society. Larvik *KUF* activities, typically, were spoken of as being part of Larvik parish activities. People liked to think of *KUF* as a branch of the parish. In point of fact, while *KUF* members belong to the Larvik parish, *KUF* was a separate entity. People paid membership dues to belong to *KUF* and Larvik *KUF* was paid a monthly allowance by the City of Larvik for the use of *KUF Huset* by the Larvik parish. (The city paid all Larvik parish expenses, except projects supported by special freewill offerings.) The Larvik parish paid rent to use *KUF Huset* once a month for a Sunday morning *Familiegudstjeneste* (Family Worship Service) and for three weekly Confirmation classes (two of which were taught by Dell). The rental agreement even included office space at *KUF Huset* for use by the Larvik pastors for pastoral counseling and office work.

KUF Huset did not serve only the Larvik parish, though. It was built by *KUF* for its own programs and activities. Of these, scouting programs and events were especially prominent. In Norway, the Boy Scout and Girl Scout organizations come in two kinds; some scouting programs are "secular" and some are "religious." *KUF* had distinctly religious scouting programs.

KUF-sponsored programs for youth and adults met at *KUF Huset*. In Larvik, these programs included Boy Scouts, Girl Scouts, Y-SING (a youth choir for teenagers), and Y'S MEN (a *KUF* men's group). In addition, Larvik *KUF* hosts regular family evening programs, weekday coffee social gatherings for senior citizens, and *Barnagospelkor* (arguably, not a *KUF* choir but a Larvik parish choir for elementary school children).

The Home Mission Society of Larvik had fewer members than *KUF*, and activities at *Bedehuset* appealed mostly to grandparents and great-grandparents. *Bedehuset* was primarily used for prayer meetings and fellowship. In the past, it also was used by the Larvik Church's Sunday School. One interesting use of *Bedehuset* was a traditional gathering of confirmands at *Bedehuset* before church on Confirmation Sunday. Each year, the Larvik Church's confirmands gathered at *Bedehuset* to put on their white robes and then they marched in a procession to Larvik Church for their Confirmation service.

The importance of *KUF* and *Indremisjonen* (The Home Mission Society) to the vitality and ministry of the Larvik parish was undeniable. The dedication we witnessed among our friends in these mission groups gave us hope in the midst of any doubts and frustrations we may otherwise have experienced as we considered the vitality of the Church of Norway and the hopefulness of its future.

We know that Larvik is not representative of all parishes in Norway. We also realize that there were dedicated Christian young people and young families in Larvik. But, to tell the truth, we perceived that the church was mainly for the elderly. This perception alarmed us, not because we do not rejoice over the faithful who attain old age, but because the faith needs a bridge over which to pass from one generation to another. We heard many older members—"pillars of the church"—say that families are too busy today for church. When grandparents make excuses for their children, however, they are destroying this very bridge which their grandchildren need for a living Christian faith.

Despite the repeated assurances of Norwegian church members—both active and less active members—that Norway has a folk church which ministers to all the people through its unique socio-religious institutional structures, we saw signs of a church with a questionable future. Why? Because so few children, youth, young adults and young families attend Sunday worship, and Sunday worship is for us a barometer by which we measure the best chances for the church's future. To suggest that the church has a vibrant future, when an average of only three percent of its membership attends church, does not make sense to us.

So, though we are not going to do anything to try change the Church of Norway, we return to our own church with a sense of alarm over the similarities between the patterns of worship attendance in Norway and those in the USA! In so many American churches, few youth and young adults attend worship. Rather than being so different from church life in the USA, it seems that Norway provides a picture of what the future holds for us if we do not do better in making the faith a vital concern for our youth.

We do not want to leave the impression that we did not see any youth ministry being done in Norway. We were impressed by the effort of the Larvik *KUF* (the Norwegian YMCA/YWCA) in its pursuit of youth ministry. In the USA, the "Y" often seems to be a health or athletic club, not a religious youth organization. The Norwegian "Y", however, had a distinctly religious orientation. We especially enjoyed the use of youth choirs by *KUF* to reach out to youth. These youth (and the confirmands who were obligated to attend a set number of services) were basically the only youth ever to attend worship. Yet, these choirs did not once sing a choir anthem during Sunday worship while we were in Larvik, although they performed elsewhere. Youth choirs, like Larvik *KUF*'s Y-SING choir, offer excellent possibilities for youth ministry in the

USA, but such choirs ought to be incorporated into the life of the congregation—especially its worship.

We also came back from Norway with a renewed concern for the importance of evangelism in the life and mission of American churches. Norway has a state church and a state church exists for all the people. Contact is made with "everyone" in school and nearly "all Norwegians" participate in weddings, baptisms, confirmation, and funerals. Virtually everyone receives Christian instruction both from the school and from the church. Children from "good church families" and children from families that have hardly any ties at all with the church, attended confirmation classes. A lot of those families, if they lived in the USA, would have had no contact whatever with a church. In Norway, virtually everyone is exposed to the gospel; that is not the case here. Probably a third or more of our population has no church connection at all. Another third probably has some affiliation with a church, but marginal at best. The question facing us is: What are we going to do to reach out to everyone with the gospel in the USA? How can we do a better job of reaching out to "the unchurched" and to "inactive church members"? Our year in Norway reminded us of just how serious a challenge we face in this regard and what happens if the challenge is not faced.

In favor of church life in the USA, the voluntary nature of congregational participation and support seems to create more commitment from church members. More people attend worship in the USA and congregations have far more church programs and activities. One of the biggest shocks was to see how tenaciously those who were active in the Norwegian church defended the status quo.

The exchange taught us both to value what we have in our USA churches and, at the same time, to be more critical of our churches. It is important to note that the effects of the exchange went beyond our family. Many others in both the Cedar Rapids and the Larvik congregations also took a fresh look at their faith and their church because of the exchange. We are confident that, as Bishop Andersen of the Tunsberg Diocese told us, "The exchange will make a difference for the church in the long run."

CHAPTER 11

OVER THE FJELL AND ACROSS THE FJORD

We were not on vacation for a year. We all worked hard and Dell had a job to do. We had the same number of weeks' vacation time that we had in Iowa. When we returned to Iowa an often asked question was, "How was your trip?" We felt a little defensive, and when the question was stated that way we stressed that we worked very hard during our time in Norway.

Once it is established that we were not on vacation for a year, we can talk about all of our wonderful experiences and vacation time. Dell had a job to do, but every day off, every weekend he did not preach, and every holiday, we squeezed in an adventure. The world was new to us and every day was special.

There are great advantages in going to a community as foreigners and being able to say, "We arrived on this date and we are going to leave on this date." In fact, we had to register with the local police and give them the date we would be leaving. The week before our departure we had to visit them again and "check out." Everyone knew when we came and exactly when we would be going back to the USA. When people said that they wanted to share an experience or their hospitality with us they followed through because they knew we would be leaving. It was not a "We'll do this someday" situation. Because of this we had some amazing experiences. We must be fair to our American friends and congregation. What happened to us was not unique to Norway. The Norwegian family in Iowa was treated exceptionally well, too. Most American pastors and families can only imagine being treated as the Isaksens were. In Norway, we also were told by clergy and spouses when we shared our adventures, that "No one has ever done that for us." The time limitation stimulated action and it continued throughout our stay. Social invitations came our first week, and the day before we left for home we were invited for lunch at the home of someone we had not met before that day.

We are amazed now that we figured out where we were supposed to be and when, especially during those first weeks. The children had school programs, scouts, swim lessons, as well as many social invitations. We were invited for coffee, afternoon and evening, the first two weeks. We were always treated extremely graciously. One afternoon we were invited for coffee at the home of a couple we had just met. We were greeted, and we sat down to have coffee at the coffee table. Of course there were candles, cut flowers, *smørbrød*, and cakes. We began a pleasant conversation, and soon found out that their 19-year-old son had been in an accident that morning and was in surgery at that time. We immediately offered to leave, but these gracious people insisted we stay, saying that our visit kept their minds off their son and that there was nothing that they could do for him at that time. That is gracious.

April passed quickly and we hardly noticed that it was a cold, dreary month. May and June were beautiful. The temperature was in the 70's and 80's and the sky was a bright cloudless blue. To a family from the Midwest the sea was a beautiful siren. We fell in love with it and during those summer days it became a part of us.

When we returned home we were often asked, "What do you miss most about Norway?" The first answer was always "our friends," but another longing was for the sea. You really cannot tell your friends in Iowa that you miss living near the sea. The days were glorious and the Norwegian people often took a few moments to lift their faces toward the sun, close their eyes and soak up the warm longed-for rays. May and June were so nice that even the Norwegians had to admit the weather was beautiful. People kept saying, "*Ja*, but by June 1 the nice weather will leave." By June 20 the warm weather continued and people told us, "*Ja*, but after June 23 (Midsummer's Eve) it will get cool." It was almost like predicting the end of the world. We sensed a little disappointment when the cool weather did not come as predicted.

One friend counted each sunny day as a blessing and offered to share Norway in its full splendor. He came to our door one day, a stranger, and said, "Tomorrow is supposed to be a beautiful day. I'd like to take your family for a boat ride on the sea." The date was May 8. We did not know we were being invited to enjoy one of the most glorious, memorable days of our lives.

The sea was calm on the day of our outing. The surface was like a mirror and it reflected all the new sights, doubling their beauty. Days like this on the sea are rare because it takes two preceeding calm days to still the water like that. We visited huge granite islands where eiderdown nests were tucked in the rocky crevices. After a picnic, we lay on the sun-baked surface of the giant grey boulders. The day was perfect. We returned home in the evening tired with that special fatigue that comes from a day in the sun and sea air.

The high point of our leisure was balanced by the reality of work. The next morning Dell had the confirmation service, on his own, in the large church. The only other time the church was as well attended was Christmas Eve.

We fondly remember the time we ate out. That sounds strange to middle America, but not in Norway. Our anniversary is May 26 and we planned ahead where we wanted to go for dinner—and we saved for it. As a source of conversation before the big outing, we asked friends where they went when they went out for a special event. Even friends we saw as financially secure could not remember the last time they had been out to eat. Some older couples went out for their anniversaries and at Christmas. We thought of our parents and stories we had heard of the "old days" when people in the USA ate out only once or twice a year. How things have changed! We believe this change will come to Norway, also. Whether it is good or bad, we do not know. We did enjoy eating out for our anniversary more that year than ever before and we savor the memory of that meal—whatever it was that we ate.

We went to a popular restaurant in a small resort community on the sea. The setting was idyllic. We phoned ahead for reservations, but to our surprise there was only one other couple in the restaurant. The tourist season had not begun. We quickly lost confidence in our language skills when we found out that the menu was written only in Norwegian and no one in the restaurant spoke English. Resorting to the pointing method of ordering, we ordered two different meals to be safe. We had two of the most delicious fish dinners we had ever eaten. We also knew it would be a long time before we ate out again. For dessert we bought an ice cream bar at the local *kiosk* and walked along the piers admiring the tall sailboats. We went home and toasted our anniversary with a glass of wine. You do not share a toast at the restaurant, one of you must be the designated driver.

Twice in June we had the opportunity to do more than admire the impressive sailboats; we spent time sailing in the Oslo *fjord*. The invitations came contingent on sun and wind; when the days came, we were provided with both. The temperature was in the 80's, we traveled between five and six knots, and the boat tipped at an angle between 15 and 22 degrees.

We sailed with two different families who loved sailing and spent most of their vacation time on sailing trips. Though summer homes are very popular in Norway, some sea-lovers purchase cruisers or sailboats with overnight accommodations as a substitute for a summer home, although a summer home is usually available to them through extended family. One family told us that they take their annual vacation on their sailboat. They purchased their sailboat with a loan and each year they make boat payments with the money that would otherwise have been spent on a family vacation or a summer cabin. This family was the third owner of this particular sailboat which was built in 1980. We discussed boat prices and learned that their boat originally cost $46,000. The second owner paid $39,000 and the current owner bought this boat in 1986 for $36,000. The boat held its value and the owner valued his leisure time spent sailing.

In a land so remote and surrounded by so much water, the sea is a source of pleasure and transportation. We combined the practical with the pleasurable. We often went to Denmark by ship to grocery shop. We really did save money by going to Denmark. Traveling on this huge ship was a mini-vacation for us, too. Does your family ever plan 24-hour getaways at the local motel to relax? Well, because of the cost, motels were out of the question, so we would get tickets on the Larvik Line and go to Denmark. The ship's name was the *Peter Wessel*. This ship sailed daily from Larvik to Denmark. When we first heard there was a ferry we expected to see a vessel much different from what we saw. The *Peter Wessel* held 650 cars and 2,200 passengers. There were restaurants, a theatre, a disco, and 530 sleeping rooms for 1,850 passengers. The sleeping rooms each had a toilet, sink, and shower. Before our first trip Ian had been worried about taking a ferry and having it sink. He was so relieved when he saw how large the *Peter Wessel* was. He said, "If that ship sinks it would still be above water." We said, "No, it wouldn't" and he replied, "Don't tell me that."

We all swallowed our fears of a sea crossing and enjoyed our trips. They were fun, but uneventful unless you count getting seasick during the winter crossings. The trip was six hours to Denmark and six hours back. Sometimes we took a one-day trip over and back. We would do some shopping, pig out on Danish pastry, buy our limit of groceries and run to catch the ferry back to Larvik. If we took a night-crossing we had a full day to shop and see some sights. In 11 months we made this trip 14 times—perhaps we broke a record.

What did we do on the long boat ride? Many people on the ship were (1) smoking and (2) drinking. There were tax-free shops on the ship and cigarettes and liquor were available. You could take only so many of these items off the ship and people wanted to take advantage of the "good deals." The children decided that the members of our family were the only ones on the ship not smoking. Wherever we went during our time in Norway we were surprised by the number of people smoking. It seems Americans have come a long way on this problem. The third vice on this beautiful, fun ship was gambling. "Gambling is bad," and we stressed this theme for the twelve hours of our first trip to Denmark. We were weak, so after a couple of trips we said, "Gambling is bad, but slot machines are fun, and they keep the kids occupied." On the Larvik Line, there were many different gambling machines and there was no age limit. At first our children just watched other people and played video games. We began to see little difference between the video games and the games that occasionally paid. The children realized that whether they played video games or slot machines they would eventually spend all their game money, but they could play slot machines longer. They had only so much money to spend. A dilemma did present itself occasionally when a child hit a small jackpot, but we worked through those problems. After Ian spent his game money he would help Norwegians, Danes, Swedes, Germans, and British who needed a game explained to them. The kids were not off gambling all the time. We relaxed, ate Danish goodies, occasionally saw a movie, read, played board games, or went to the top deck to enjoy the sunshine. We always arrived home with our limit of imported food; the mini-getaway was also an economic blessing.

When we first arrived we rediscovered the pleasure of walking. We walked not only for leisure, but as transportation. Unless we left town, we walked most places. We came to appreciate walking as a time to talk with each other or just a time to collect our thoughts between activities. Time to think is an important part of life. We walked the hilly streets of Larvik daily, our muscles getting stronger and the distances we walked increasing.

Most evenings (even throughout the mild winter) we went for a walk to debrief and make plans; we also enjoyed looking into the brightly lit rooms of the homes we passed. Certain decorating themes were repeated. Walls were often covered with paintings, candles, and all kinds of different wall plates. Often the paintings were original works, not prints. A fortune in art? Most often the paintings were painted by Grandpa, Great Uncle or someone in the family. They were usually very nice. We decided that it is difficult to live with so much natural beauty around and not want to try capture it. Diane fell in love with the lace valances in the windows, the flowers on the window sill, and the small light hanging down the center of the window. The single light replaced the traditional single candle once burned in the window of Scandinavian homes as a symbol of welcome.

We walked a lot, but we did not willingly walk in the rain— another sign of our being Americans. Norwegian children walked to school in the rain and played outside in the rain. Once we saw a group of preschoolers at a day care center out for recess on a rainy day. They were covered from head to toe in their rain gear.

We were invited on a day-long outing to pick *tyttebær* (lingonberries) and *blåbær* (blueberries) in the mountains of Telemark in the fall. The forecast was for rain and we were asked if we had brought all our rain gear from the USA. They meant hooded jacket, rain pants and rain boots for five people. We didn't own rain pants and boots; even if we did they would not have fit in our limited luggage. We borrowed all that we needed and enjoyed a day outdoors despite the rain. We purchased beautiful Helly Hansen rain jackets for each child. They were proud to wear them to school in Norway, but back home in Iowa we had to insist that they wear them on a rainy day—they preferred to run from one dry place to another like everyone else.

People tried to figure out why we didn't bring our rain gear, and then we admitted that we didn't even bring our skis and boots. Again, someone worked to find the proper fit for five pairs of skis and boots. Norway is the home of skiing and everyone skis. Skiing in Scandinavia goes back about 4,000 years. It was not for recreation, but for transporation. Immigrants to the USA introduced Americans to skiing, cross-country skiing. Downhill skiing, alpine skiing, or *slalåm* as it is called in Norway, came later. We were surprised when some very elderly people told us that they still skied. We found out that when people talked about skiing generally they meant cross-country skiing. But, as you think of those wide, flat stretches of land in Minnesota or Iowa, remember cross-country in Norway is like downhill skiing in some of our states. The first week in December we got a foot and a half of snow on Friday night. By Sunday afternoon the warm sun was melting the snow quickly. We were anxious to try skiing and did. The icy snow brought us down the hills very quickly and made walking up the next hill without falling down very difficult. We were looking forward to the next snowfall that would stay soft for a few days. With promises of more snow we looked forward to skiing a few times in January and February. So, we leaned our five pairs of skis in the corner of the entry room of our home to be used another day. The snow never came and the next time we moved the skis was to return them to their owners the week before we left.

We enjoyed the mild winter, but the absence of white snow on the ground made the long winter days even darker. The lack of television made the dark days seem even longer. It is amazing how far you can get in a novel in one evening. We all read a lot. There was no TV during the day; programming in the evening was poor. We got one Norwegian station and two Swedish stations. One night Bethany was bored and we found her watching a German movie with Swedish subtitles. We tried to watch some Norwegian TV, but a half hour of focusing on a flower or a waterfall with classical music in the background did not excite us. There were some American reruns, but most of the American movies that were shown were so bad we doubt that they were ever shown here. At night X-rated Norwegian and Swedish films were on TV. A friend told us that one night she stayed up to watch a movie. She was alone in her own home and she said it still made her blush.

We read, we played cards, we listened to music, the children did homework, and we wrote letters. Friday nights would come and we felt the need to be entertained rather than entertain ourselves. We would rent a VCR and videos. We were vulnerable, and it was fun. From the time we arrived in Larvik to the time we left there was an increase in the number of movies available on videotape. We probably paid enough in VCR rental fees to buy a VCR back home.

(We were disappointed when the VCR we rented didn't allow us to play back the videotaped messages sent to us by friends back in Iowa. American and European televisions operate with two different systems.)

We had a little trouble picking out movies. We started out depending on the rating system, but we found that ratings were culturally based and we had to rate the movies ourselves. In Norway, a movie with bad language and explicit sex could be rated for 10-year-olds or 12-year-olds; there was a different rating for each of these ages. A violent movie rated PG and PG-13 back home could be rated for 18-year-olds in Norway. The children went to the movie theatre a few times with friends. It was interesting to us that the theatre was closed Saturday nights. People were proud to tell us that their movies were not dubbed and they only use subtitles. Because of this, Norwegian kids are learning American English very fast.

For a pastor's family, the church in the USA provides many social gatherings. The Norwegian church is not set up for this. *KUF* (YMCA) provided some social functions, but we were still working hard to reconcile the idea that the YMCA was part of the church. The members of *KUF* were wonderful and we believe that, in time, the strangeness of this situation would have worn off. We had fun social times with people from *KUF*. At one picnic, Bethany played the piano and we taught the people the song, "We are the Church," in English. Another time we gathered at the summer home of a family for fellowship and games. There were some Sunday night events; we attended most, but we never figured out if these were church events and if the pastor was expected to show up.

Some women from the Larvik parish started a Bible School in a community room of nearby apartments. It sounded strange to us, but they wanted to reach out to these children who received religious education only in the school. Diane visited this group once, and on another occasion Dell and Megan visited them and taught them the song, "God is so good," in Norwegian. They enjoyed learning a new song and music was such a wonderful way to share our common faith in Jesus Christ.

The choir Bethany belonged to, Y-SING, also was a Christian youth group. It is difficult for us to imagine a group of teenagers planning their own fellowship events. For New Year's Eve, they planned a dinner, games, and went as a group to the midnight worship service at the Larvik Church. They were extremely self-motivated and planned fun events and fundraisers, as a Christian youth group.

Friends, as well as people involved in mission groups, met for Bible study. Dell and Diane joined one such group which met monthly in each other's home for dinner and Bible study. We enjoyed the fellowship we experienced with this group. The group chose their own discussion material and faithfully studied the lesson. Sometimes the material contained radical and challenging discussion ideas. We jotted down some interesting statistics that came up during one lesson. The religious beliefs of Norwegians and Americans were compared.

COMPARISON OF RELIGIOUS BELIEFS IN NORWAY AND THE USA[4]

RELIGIOUS BELIEF IN...	NORWAY	USA
...God	70%	95%
...Life after death	42%	71%
...Devil	27%	66%
...Hell	21%	67%
...Heaven	46%	84%

The local *Indremisjonen* (Home Mission Society) included many good and faithful people. The average age of the membership was quite high. Every Friday night they had services. They faithfully passed out fliers at the elementary school each Friday inviting the children to attend. Megan and Ian decided to go one Friday night. A friend of Ian's, who had never attended church before, decided to go with them. As with most Norwegian services and meetings the service was long. The children came home saying it was boring and that they would never go again. Still the evening had some benefit; the next day Ian's friend asked him many questions about God. Later that day Ian came home very excited. He said, "Petter says that he believes in God now because I do." We believe the children had many opportunities to be witnesses, by their lives, by their actions, and by informal testimonies of their faith.

Life in Larvik, Norway, was the main event. It was not a year-long vacation, but it was wonderful. We did, however, take a family vacation. We realize that vacations are for those experiencing them and most people would be happier if everyone saw vacations as a private part of life. We will be brief and avoid telling you about each tourist stop along our trip. We chose to stay in Scandinavia. Having limited time and money we had to decide between seeing many countries in southern Europe, or three countries in northern Europe. Because we were living in Norway we wanted the children to become better acquainted with this area. Soon after arriving in Larvik we had to choose a vacation date. We struggled with the calendar and suggested some dates to the church staff. The weeks off that we proposed were met with wrinkled brows of bewilderment and statements like, "Well, I suppose that could work out." We went back to the calendar. Eventually, we suggested three weeks in July. Smiles followed, and we realized we had gotten it right. July is the time when everyone goes on holiday or vacation.

We set off from Larvik in July with five loaded down backpacks and five train passes. We explored Oslo, then headed north to Trondheim. We went to Røros where we were met by Larvik friends who took us to their summer home in the mountains. We relaxed, visited a goat farm, swam in the icy water of a nearby river, and enjoyed fresh trout dinners. One morning before anyone else was up, Ian and the Norwegian daughter his age got fishing poles and went fishing. Proud of their catch, they provided us fresh fish for breakfast.

We returned to Oslo by train, then continued on to Bergen. The scenery of this trip was so overwhelmingly beautiful that we almost became numb to it after hours on the train.

The train took us back to Oslo again and we continued on to Stockholm. The children were willing to balance tours of museums and palaces with amusement parks and a zoo. The cities also gave us a chance to admit that we missed an occasional fast food meal.

In Oslo at McDonalds we had two Big Macs, three fish sandwiches, five french fries and five Cokes for $40. We enjoyed it and it was the best deal around.

We tried to combine culture, fun, history, and meaningfulness during this vacation. From Stockholm we went to a small town to meet and visit with Diane's Swedish relatives. We got to visit the farm where her great-grandparents lived before moving to the USA. We also stopped at the church where they were married.

We moved on to Copenhagen, and we were getting tired. In Copenhagen we enjoyed the hospitality of some people we had met back in Larvik. We had tried to plan the trip so that we could be at Tivoli amusement park on Bethany's 14th birthday. We were on schedule and had a fun day doing what the kids liked to do— play. We saw what most tourists see in Copenhagen, then headed back to Larvik to rest and wash clothes. Back in Larvik for only half a day, we were invited to someone's summer home for the afternoon. We squeezed it in and early the next morning we were on the train to Stavanger.

Dell's family had come from near Stavanger, an island called Rennesøy. We stayed on a neighboring island in the summer home of some other Larvik friends. On the island, friends of our friends' friends heard that we wanted to get to Rennesøy and appeared with a boat to take us. We hope you realize by now how often people came forward to help us out. We went to meet Dell's Norwegian relatives. The organist from the Larvik church had relatives in Stavanger. He had his brother put an advertisement in the paper to help us locate these people. They answered the ad. The Larvik organist was surprised to find out that he and Dell were 9th cousins. While we visited these Norwegian relatives on Rennesøy they brought out a book with names of other American family members. We found out that members of our first parish in Minnesota were related to Dell. Amazing. Through the kindness of the present occupants we got to walk through the home of Dell's great-great grandfather. They did not know how old the house was, but it had been moved onto that site in 1730.

Traveling was wonderful, but after traveling 3,000 miles by train we were happy to be going home and Larvik was home. When we returned it felt so natural to be there, so right. It is always nice to get home after a trip.

We had saved three vacation days for the first week in August. The last week in July was cool and rainy and we thought summer was over. We were invited to spend three days at the senior pastor's wife's family's summer home on an island near Arendal. The morning we left Larvik the sky was clear and the sun was warm. The three days we spent on this island were cloudless and in the 80's. There was a big old frame home without electricity or plumbing. The house was filled with the pastor's children, grandchildren, and our family. Pastor Bolstad, the senior pastor, called this summer home "Paradise" and it certainly was. While we were there, it was sunny and warm, with just enough breeze to move the children's homemade sailboat in a protected channel between two islands in the sea. Like so many places we had seen that summer in Scandinavia, it was paradise. Unfortunately, there are too few perfect sunny days "in paradise."

CHAPTER 12

YES, WE LOVE THIS LAND

Where were we for this year?

Norwegians are quick to say that Norway is not the capital of Sweden. We thought that was a cute little joke until we returned home and received many letters from friends saying they hoped we had a good year in Sweden.

Norway is an independent nation, but we were surprised to learn that they have been independent only since 1905. At that time they asked Prince Carl of Denmark to become their king. He changed his name to Haaken VII, and took his wife and two-year-old son with him to Norway. Norway has a constitutional monarchy with the king as head of State. The parliament is called the *Storting* and is headed by an elected prime minister.

Haaken VII's young son, Prince Alexander Edward Christian

Fredrik, was born in England. After coming to Norway his name was changed to Olav V. Olav ruled Norway as king for 33 years until his death on January 17, 1991. He was 87. King Olav was called "*Folkekongen,*" the people's king. He was a king in the hearts of the Norwegian people. Olav became king when his father died; a consecration service was held at Nidaros Cathedral in Trondheim on June 22, 1958. It was his wish to be blessed for his task as king. His wife, Martha, had died in 1954; they had three children. Their son, Harald V, became King of Norway after his father's death. Harald's ascension to the throne was very significant because when Harald was born in 1937 it had been 566 years since a Norwegian prince had been born in Norway.

We journeyed to Decorah, Iowa, to see King Olav four months before we left for Norway. The timing was fortuitous. The excitement stirred by seeing the king helped us get through the piles of work in preparation. The children promptly wrote their Norwegian penpals and said, "We've seen your king!" In Norway people always spoke with affection for Olav. He was the second king to rule modern Norway and a symbol of their nationhood. He was important to them. Many Norwegians did not know where Iowa was, but we could tell them that their king knew—we had seen him there.

There are over 4 million Norwegians in Norway. The population is about the same as Minnesota and the land area is 125,000 square miles, about the same as New Mexico. The land is not compact— it stretches 1,100 miles from Kirkenes in the north to Lindesnes in the south. Southern Norway is closer to the French Riviera than it is to Kirkenes. The coastline of Norway is broken by hundreds of *fjords* or fingerlike projections of water jutting into the land. The Sognefjord near Bergen is 114 miles long. If the coast of Norway were straightened out it would reach halfway around the world. The coast is dotted with about 50,000 islands. About 2,000 of them are inhabited. When we think of Norway we think of rock, water, and trees: 70% of the land is mountains; 22%, forests; 5%, lakes and rivers; and only 3% is soil for cultivation.

One third of Norway extends beyond the Arctic Circle. Southern Norway is about the same latitude as Juneau, Alaska. Because of the Gulf Stream, the warm tropical ocean-river, the coasts of Norway are kept ice free. For this reason, Norway has relied on the sea for her economy. Most of the population of Norway lives within 12 miles of the sea.

In the past, whaling, fishing, and shipping were the main occupations. Today the main economic base is fishing (cod or *torsk* and herring are the most important fish), agriculture, forestry (pulp, paper and building materials), oil, gas and hydroelectricity. Although the whaling industry has died out, due to its active whaling industry in the past, Norway has a bad reputation among groups concerned with saving the whales. God's gifts—the forests, the mountains and waterfalls, the sea and the oil beneath the sea— provide Norway's wealth.

Norway has a social welfare system that provides cradle-to-grave protection. Norwegians see themselves as a victimless, humanitarian society. The people are secure and have a very high standard of living. They pay for their security with taxes, over one-third of their income goes for taxes. Because of high taxes and a great value placed on leisure time, it can be debated whether or not the Norwegian worker today works as hard as he or she might. The average work week is 37 hours, and the production worker in Norway is paid the highest wage of production workers anywhere in the world—$18.92 an hour in 1990.

The four largest cities in Norway are Oslo, Bergen, Trondheim, and Stavanger. Stavanger is the boom town oil city. There are American oil companies in Stavanger and Americans living there. There was one grocery store that sold American products. We arrived in Stavanger on a Friday afternoon and discovered this store five minutes before closing time. We bought what we needed for supper before catching the ferry to the island where we were staying. We were so excited about this discovery. At last we could buy "real" mustard and Miracle Whip. The next morning we arrived with our wish list of longed-for foods to take back to Larvik. The store was closed and did not open until 10:00 a.m., Monday morning. Our train left at 8:00 a.m. We passed that store often that weekend—pressing five noses to the glass to catch a glimpse of the treats in the store. If the store had been open we would have paid high prices for our "wants." We met an American woman who had lived in Stavanger for a few years. She told us that her first months there she became very depressed after each grocery shopping trip and that was at a regular Norwegian grocery store. After that, her husband did all the shopping. We visited the Stavanger Cathedral—a church dedicated in 1125.

Trondheim was the capital of Norway in the 1200's. The kings of Norway are crowned in the largest medieval building in Scandinavia—Nidaros Cathedral. It is an impressive building and we almost missed seeing the inside. The day we had planned to see Nidaros Cathedral there was a bomb threat. We rearranged our day and returned later in the afternoon to tour the inside of the famous cathedral. We had not expected a bomb threat at a cathedral in Norway. New York City, on the other hand, averages 13 bomb scares a day.

Bergen is the Hanseatic city on the west coast. A strong German influence dates back to the 14th century when the *Hanse* (German merchants) set up shop in Bergen. When we studied language tapes before leaving the USA we learned to say, "It always rains in Bergen." When we walked through the city we saw remnants of broken umbrellas on the sidewalks and in gutters along the streets. We even saw umbrella repair shops. Bergen's setting is beautiful and we thought if we could only see it when the sun was shining it must be one of the prettiest cities in the world. To get to Bergen you travel through a fairyland of rugged mountains, *fjords*, valleys, and cascading waterfalls: the land of trolls and *The Three Billy Goats Gruff*.

Oslo is the capital city of Norway. To us it felt more like a big small town than a capital city. There are about 450,000 people in this city. In terms of land mass (182 square miles) Oslo is one of the top 10 largest cities in the world. It is a large city for only 450,000 people which suits the Norwegian love of nature and recreation. Some famous landmarks in Oslo are Frogner Park, Akershus, and the museums of Bygdøy. Holmenkollen ski jump was used in the 1952 Winter Olympics and stands high above the city.

Frogner Park is an open-air museum with 175 sculptures of

granite, bronze, and iron by Gustav Vigeland. His controversial works are greeted with divided reactions by both Norwegians and visitors. The central figure is a 52-foot-high monolith of 121 intertwining figures representing the struggle of life.

Akershus Castle is a fortress built in 1300. On the grounds is a resistance museum dedicated to Norwegian patriots, many of whom were executed here during the Nazi occupation of World War II. The museum chronicles events of World War II in Norway from the German invasion in 1940 to liberation in 1945.

In Oslo on the Bygdøy Peninsula there are five museums. The Viking Ship Museum contains three burial ships from Viking times, archeological finds from the shores of the Oslo *fjord*. The museum also displays a collection of objects found in one of the ships, the Oseberg ship.

The Fram Museum has the polar ship built by Colin Archer and used by Fridtjof Nansen to sail across the Arctic in 1893-1896. Later, Roald Amundsen sailed the Fram to the South Pole and became the first man to reach the South Pole in 1911.

The Kon-Tiki Museum holds the balsa wood raft, the Kon-Tiki. Thor Heyerdahl sailed the Kon-Tiki from Peru to Polynesia in 1947. Also in this museum is the papyrus Ra II, a vessel in which Thor Heyerdahl crossed the Atlantic from Morocco to Barbados.

The Norwegian Maritime Museum has an exhibition showing the maritime history of Norway.

The Folk Museum has 170 old buildings that have been reassembled on Bygdøy. The buildings are grouped according to the regions they are from in Norway. Some of the buildings date back to the Middle Ages. There is a stave church from around the year 1200. There is a variety of rural architecture represented because the villages were widely scattered and isolated before mass communication.

The stave church in the Folk Museum is from Gol in Hallingdal. The stave church is built of strong pillars or staves. The staves stand on solid ground and hold the roof. The walls are upright boards that fit into frames. There are no windows. The largest stave church or *stavkirke* is at Heddal in Telemark. The stave churches have an Oriental look with dragon heads on the roof. The dragon was a symbol used for evil before Christianity. The dragons on these early churches were symbols of God's protection against evil.

Some modern day evils plague Norway. Three environmental problems often came up in our conversations with Norwegians. The nuclear accident at Chernobyl, USSR, in 1986 left radioactive material in the soil of some areas in Norway. Grazing areas for livestock were also affected by the nuclear fallout. Another problem was acid rain produced by pollution from Great Britian and other industrialized nations. Because of acid rain, many of the beautiful lakes in Norway were dead or dying. The third environmental concern was a massive algae bloom in the North Sea during the spring of 1988, while we were in Larvik. This algae bloom threatened marine life along Norway's coast. The sunny, warm spring days we enjoyed so much triggered the algae growth. About 700 fish farms in Norway were endangered by the moving algae tide. Many fish were rescued by huge towing operations that moved the fish pens into the *fjords*. Some said that the algae bloom was common all over the world, others said it was a result of the increase of pollutants: human waste, fertilizers and industrial waste. Norwegian people were extremely concerned and supported government efforts to protect the environment. New problems were disrupting an old society.

North of Larvik is Tunsberg, the oldest city in Norway. It was founded in 872. The first time we visited the museum in Tunsberg, it was closed; however, our host made a comment to the right person and the doors were opened for us to see the museum. Of special interest to us was the skeleton of a blue whale. Some of these whales reached 150 tons; the skeleton in the museum was gigantic. The children were amazed by the size and decided that Jonah could have lived inside this whale very comfortably for three days.

The cities of Norway were fun to visit, but of course our favorite was "The Gateway to the Riviera of the North"—Larvik. The stretch from Larvik to Nevlunghavn, with its beaches on the sea, was an oasis for Norwegian vacationers.

The Larvik *fjord*, which is much different from the mountain-lined *fjords* of the west coast, came up to the city. The city is on the innermost part of the Larvik *fjord*. Larvik is on the side of a hill and reminded us of Duluth, Minnesota, only smaller. The northwest boundary is covered by a lovely beech forest. This beech forest is the northern-most beech forest in the world and the largest in Norway. The people of Larvik are very proud of it. The forest is called *Bøkeskogen*. All year it was a popular destination; people strolled there in the summer and skied in the winter. The forest belongs to the people and cannot be sold. On holidays people gathered for worship services or celebrations. On Whitmonday (the Monday after Pentecost Sunday), Dell preached at the worship service in a clearing in the woods. There were picnic tables; after the worship service, everyone brought out a tablecloth, coffee thermos, *smørbrød* and *boller* and enjoyed a social time. During the summer months in the beech forest a band played chorale music in the bandstand every Sunday morning at 9:00. It was a wonderful spot to meet people and to enjoy your Sunday morning coffee.

Larvik was a city of 8,000 inhabitants. In 1988, five municipalities incorporated to become new or greater Larvik; a city of 38,000 people.

Before we left Larvik, both the congregation and the confirmation class gave us gifts made of a special blue rock called Larvikitt. This granite rock, also called Blue Pearl, has a shiny blue surface. It is mined in the Larvik area, and is used as facade stones for buildings. Perhaps the most famous building where it has been used is the U.N. building in New York.

To the north of Larvik is the Lågen River and the Lågen Valley. In the valley is the Hedrum Church built in 1050. The farmland in this valley was rich, the farms were well-kept and picturesque. We never saw junk and old machinery lying around the farms. The prosperous looking white frame farmhouses and newly painted red barns could cause the sons and daughters of Norwegian immigrant farmers in the USA to emigrate back to Norway. We actually saw a new wooden barn being built; a rare sight in the

USA these days. The farmers were heavily subsidized by the government.

Salmon populate the Lågen River and provide a popular sport as well as a livlihood. The river flows past Larvik on the east and flows on to meet the sea.

Coming up to Larvik on the west side of the city is Lake Farris, a seven-mile long lake. At Larvik the lake is used by the family-owned Treschow Fritzøe lumber industry. This company belongs to a very "old" family. This family owns the forests that extend 45 miles (a total of 151,000 acres, including 114,000 acres of productive forests) north to south around Larvik. Studying the history of this timber company is quite an interesting way to understand Larvik itself. The first saw mill in the area was erected in 1540! A son (Ulrik Frederik Gyldenløve) of a Danish king (King Fredrik the Third) bought these estates in 1670. He founded the city of Larvik and built the Larvik Church. From here, Gyldenløve served as the Danish governor over all Norway (Norway was under Danish rule for four hundred years). After the Danes no longer controlled Norway (but "gave" Norway to Sweden against the will of the Norwegians, who wanted to be self-ruled and declared themselves such on May 17, 1814), these estates were acquired by the noble family named Treschow in 1835. The Treschow family continues to own this land and the many related subsidiary companies.

The Treschow family home, Fritzøe House, is an estate with a palace-like home on the outskirts of Larvik. Nanna Treschow, the family matriarch, attended the Langestrand Church and was very active in church leadership. Each year she hosted a gathering of clergy at her home. Every other year the spouses were invited. Diane was lucky because we were there during "the year of the spouses." Thirty-five clergy couples, the bishop, former bishop and various other local church leaders were invited for an evening of socializing, food, and music. Since our arrival in Larvik we had tried hard to get a glimpse of the mansion as we drove by; it was fun to anticipate an evening there as invited guests. The evening was special for Norwegian clergy, too. The joke of the evening was that the Shiells should have brought a camera to take pictures of the mansion and tell their congregation in Iowa that this was their

Norwegian home. (And people say Norwegians do not have a sense of humor!) The evening was elegant and certainly different from our usual church social gatherings. After refreshments, the evening continued in a room lined with paintings. We were all seated and enjoyed a piano solo played in the universal language of music.

On a tour of Larvik, the church was a special stop. The Larvik church sat on an incredible piece of property by the sea. The church was usually one of the first buildings built whenever a city was founded. A friend told us that when his children were young and their family was traveling, they always looked for the churchyard to have a picnic. It was always the nicest spot in town.

In Larvik there is a large wooden manor house—the second largest frame structure in Norway. This house was originally built in the 1670's as the home of Ulrik Frederik Gyldenløve. At one time this building was the high school in Larvik and the home of Elisabeth Hysing. Her father was the principal of the high school. Elisabeth married Vilhelm Koren. Vilhelm accepted a call to serve a pioneer Lutheran congregation in the American frontier of Iowa. They left Norway and immigrated to the USA. Vilhelm Koren later became president of the Iowa District, president of the Norwegian Synod and played a major role in founding Luther College at Decorah, Iowa.

We had never heard of Elisabeth Koren before coming to Larvik. The wife of the present principal of the Larvik high school gave Diane a copy of Mrs. Koren's published diary to read. Elisabeth Koren told the story of a pastor and his wife leaving Larvik, Norway, and settling in Iowa. We were living in Larvik; Dell was serving the church Elisabeth had attended and we had just left our home in Iowa. Before *Syttende Mai* we heard people in Larvik ask each other, "Will the trees in the beech forest—*Bøkeskogen*—have leaves this year by the Seventeenth of May?" This was a part of them—to gaze at the forest and wonder; to ponder this question each year. As Diane read Elizabeth Koren's diary she could understand Elizabeth's homesickness as she wrote one spring day in the 1850's, in a letter to her father, the familiar words, "Is the beech wood in leaf for the Seventeenth of May this year?"[5]

While in Larvik, we could understand Elisabeth Koren's longing for *Bøkeskogen*—the beech forest—because we were enjoying the beauty of her home. Iowa does not have the splendor of Norway, but at the end of our stay we understood Elisabeth's homesickness. Dorothy's voice from *The Wizard of Oz* kept going through our heads, "There's no place like home. There's no place like home." We were ready to go home.

Americans were seen as very open and generous people. Those of you who have entertained Norwegian family and friends are remembered fondly by them. The vastness of our country astounds them. (No doubt, you've had to explain that you cannot drive from New York to California to Florida in a week.) People were always anxious to tell us about their wonderful trips to the USA. On one occasion a little girl was standing nearby and overheard someone expanding on how marvelous the USA was. The little girl came up and said, "Norway is nice, too." Yes, it is. It is a beautiful country with wonderful people. We long for it with an ache. It became a second home to us and we will always live with a heart divided between the two countries. So, yes, Kristina; Norway is nice too. *Ja, vi elsker dette landet.* Yes, we love this land.

The Shiell Family

NOTES

1. This English translation of the Order of Service for the Church of Norway is based on the service in *Ordning for høymessen*, (Oslo: Verbum Forlag [Andaktsbokselskapet], 1983).

2. Usually, six hymns are sung during the service. Also, it is customary to sing all the verses. Some hymns have only a couple verses, but hymns with between six and eight verses are common.

3. Einar Haugen, *Norwegian-English Dictionary*, (Madison, Wisconsin: The University of Wisconsin Press, 1986), p. 452.

4. Sindre Eide, *Så langt, men ikke lenger: Menigheten— bare for spesielt interesserte?*, (Oslo: Verbum Andaktsbokselskapet, 1987), p. 47.

5. *The Diary of Elisabeth Koren, 1853-55*, trans. and ed. David T. Nelson, (Decorah, Iowa: Norwegian- American Museum and Luther College, 1985), p. 360.

ACKNOWLEDGEMENTS

With permission of Verbum Forlag (Andaktsbokselskapet) to print an adaptation and translation of the following copyrighted materials as they originally appear in Norwegian:

Ordning for høymessen, (Oslo: Verbum Forlag [Andaktsbokselskapet], 1983).

Sindre Eide, Så langt, men ikke lenger; Menigheten - bare for spesielt interesserte?, (Oslo: Verbum Andaktsbokselskapet, 1987), p.47.

We thank Alice Manker, Mark Schultz, and Peggy Schultz for their assistance as editors.

About The Authors

Dell and Diane Shiell are from Minneapolis, Minnesota. Both Diane and Dell received their bachelor degrees (Bachelor of Science and Bachelor of Arts, respectively) from the University of Minnesota. Dell received two post graduate degrees (Master of Divinity and Doctor of Ministry) from Luther Northwestern Seminary, St. Paul, Minnesota.

The Shiells have three children, Bethany, Megan, and Ian.

The Shiell family has lived in three communities where Dell served as parish pastor: Porter, Minnesota, Cedar Rapids, Iowa, and Venice, Florida. During 1988-1989, the Shiell family lived in Larvik, Norway, where Dell served the Larvik and Langestrand Churches. Currently, Dell is the pastor at Our Savior Lutheran Church, Venice, Florida.

In 1991, Diane and Dell founded St. Hans Ministry Exchange, Inc., a non-profit organization to promote ministry exchanges.

St. Hans Ministry Exchange, Inc.

Preparing the way for ministry exchanges
LOOKING FOR AN ADVENTURE?

Do you dream of exchanging lives with someone in another country for 6-12 months? Would you prefer to exchange your ministry setting with someone elsewhere in the USA for 6-8 weeks? St. Hans Ministry Exchange, Inc. is a non-profit organization dedicated to help such persons realize their dreams. Please complete the order from below and mail it to:

St. Hans Ministry Exchange, Inc.
P.O. Box 1041
Venice, FL. 34284-1041

— —

ORDER FORM

Send me _____ copies of
Fair Exchange at $12.95 each $ _____
    (add $2.00 each for postage/handling.) $ _____
                                              TOTAL $ _____

☐   Send me additional information
     about ministry exchanges.

If you request information please indicate if you are:
☐   Clergy   Church Affiliation _____
☐   Lay associate minister
☐   Laity   _____
☐   Other (please specify)
TO: (Please Print)

Name _____

Address _____

City/State/Zip _____

Make check or money order payable to:
St. Hans Ministry Exchange, Inc.

Radical Healing

DAVE WILLIAMS

Radical Healing

25 Miracle Keys For
Your Healing And Health

DAVE WILLIAMS

Radical Healing
25 Miracle Keys For Your Healing And Health

Unless otherwise noted, Scripture quotations are taken from the HOLY BIBLE, NEW INTERNATIONAL VERSION ®. Copyright ©1973, 1978, 1984 by International Bible Society. Used by permission of Zondervan Publishing House. All rights reserved.

Scripture quotations noted TLB are from *The Living Bible*, Copyright ©1971. Used by permission of Tyndale House Publishers, Inc., Wheaton, Illinois 60189. All rights reserved.

ISBN 0-938020-70-6

First Printing 2003

Cover Design: Gerard R. Jones

Published by

DECAPOLIS
PUBLISHING
Printed in the United States of America

BOOKS BY DAVE WILLIAMS

ABCs of Success & Happiness
The AIDS Plague
Angels: They Are Watching You!
The Art of Pacesetting Leadership
The Beauty of Holiness
The Christian Job Hunter's Handbook
Depression: Cave of Torment
The Desires of Your Heart
Developing the Spirit of a Conqueror
Filled: With the Mightiest Power in the Universe
Genuine Prosperity, The Power To Get Wealth
Getting To Know Your Heavenly Father
Gifts That Shape Your Life and Change Your World
The Grand Finale Revival
Grief and Mourning
Growing Up in Our Father's Family
Have You Heard From the Lord Lately?
How to Be a High Performance Believer
The Laying On of Hands
Lonely in the Midst of a Crowd
Miracle Results of Fasting
The New Life . . . The Start of Something Wonderful
The Pastor's Minute
The Pastor's Pay
Patient Determination
The Presence Of God
Radical Fasting
Regaining Your Spiritual Momentum
The Road To Radical Riches
The Secret of Power With God
Seven Signposts on the Road to Spiritual Maturity
Slain in the Spirit — Real or Fake?
Somebody Out There Needs You
Success Principles From the Lips of Jesus
Supernatural Soulwinning
Understanding Spiritual Gifts
What To Do If You Miss The Rapture
The World Beyond — The Mysteries Of Heaven
Your Pastor: A Key To Your Personal Wealth

Contents

Introduction 11

Chapter 1: How To Be Radically Healed 19

Chapter 2: How To Be Radically Healed, Part II 31

Chapter 3: What Causes Sickness? 39

Chapter 4: Demons And Sickness 57

Chapter 5: Why Some Stay Sick 65

Chapter 6: How People Become Sickness Magnets ... 73

Chapter 7: Twenty-Five Helps For Radical Healing 87

Chapter 8: Helps for Radical Healing, Part II 95

Chapter 9: Helps for Radical Healing, Part III 103

Chapter 10: Helps for Radical Healing, Part IV 107

Chapter 11: Helps for Radical Healing, Part V 113

Chapter 12: Helps for Radical Healing, Part VI 119

The Last Word 127

Everywhere Jesus went,
He left a trail of healed
people in His wake.

Introduction

The lady sitting in my office was one of the goofi-est people I had ever met. Not only did she talk in-cessantly, but I could hardly follow her train of thought. I looked across the room at my associate pastor, Dave Snook, and rolled my eyes. He rolled his eyes back at me, and I asked myself again as the woman droned on, "Why did I let her into my of-fice?"

The months leading up to that day had been tor-ture — pure torture. I had been pastor for three years, and the pressures of the "job" were catching up with me. I developed such pain in my chest that I could barely breathe at times. I would feel electrical cur-rents run down my left arm, and I was scared that I was going to have a stroke. My dad had died of heart trouble at the age of forty, and his father had died at an early age of a stroke. The devil had always told me it would happen to me too. I felt I was under the curse of bad genes.

Looking back, now, I can see that the pains were caused by my inexperience. I did nothing right to maintain my health during those early years of pastoring. On Monday there was always a deacon in my office telling me everything I did wrong on Sunday (I should have learned to shun his meetings). I wasn't eating right or exercising, and I was totally focused on the ministry with few other outlets. I wanted so much to be a good pastor, but I simply didn't know how to handle the challenges.

One night, a few weeks before my visit with the strange lady, I was on my way home from church. Suddenly it felt like an elephant was standing on my chest. I kept the car on the road as the currents began running down my left arm. Slowly, it became almost numb. Beads of sweat dripped down my body. "This is it," I thought. "I'm coming home, Lord!"

By the time I arrived at my house, I was sweating and crying, gripped with this unknown pain. My wife, Mary Jo, told me to go to the emergency room, but I stubbornly refused. I kept praying, "God, You said I shall live and not die. I don't know what's wrong, so please send somebody who can help me." Before we all went to bed, I said good-bye to my family (just in case). Somehow I made it through the night.

The next day the pain had lessened, but it was not the last time I would face it. Over the months, it came and went until one Wednesday when I got a call from a missionary friend in nearby Grand Rapids. I shouldn't have been in the office that day because the pain the night before had been more than I could bear, and I hadn't slept. But I was there to receive the call. What he said caught me off guard.

"Dave, there's a lady from Tulsa, Oklahoma, here who says God sent her to Michigan to pray for a pastor, and *you* are that pastor," he said. "She couldn't get in to Lansing because of weather, but she's in Grand Rapids. Can I bring her over?"

I thought it was a strange situation, but I agreed. A little while later he brought the woman into the church, and she looked at me and said, "Hi, honey." I had never seen her before. "Hello," I said.

"I'm Eunice, an evangelist from Tulsa," she said. "God sent me here to pray for you."

I invited her to sit down, and I had Dave Snook, my associate pastor, join us. "Dave," I said, "meet Evangelist Eunice from Tulsa." Eunice looked at Dave and said, "Hi, honey." She began to chat, and after a while, we were wondering what kind of nut she was. Her manner, her conversation, and even the way she had come to be in Lansing were odd.

Had she really heard from God about praying for me? Or had I invited a wacko into my office to waste my time?

Then, all of a sudden, in the middle of this strange monologue, she stopped. Her eyes got big, and she walked toward me, came behind my desk, swung my swivel chair around, and put her hands on my chest. I had not told her a thing about myself because she hadn't let anyone else speak. Nobody knew about the chest pains but my wife.

"In the Name of Jesus, I call for a total healing of this heart and all the arteries," she said and started prophesying. I sat there, caught off guard, while she continued. Then she said, "There."

I did not feel anything except surprised. But she wasn't finished.

She looked at Dave Snook and said, "God's got something for you too." I could almost see Dave as he tried to slink out of the room! As a conservative person, he didn't go for spiritual displays. When somebody would be slain in the Spirit during a service, he would often look at me and roll his eyes. He believed it was an emotional response or something people faked.

Eunice reached her hand up and touched Dave on the chin, and Dave, who had been standing, hit the ground like a two-by-four. He lay half in my office and half in my secretary's office and started turning blue and yellow, and shivering as if he were cold. Eunice motioned me over and said, "Feel his leg." I obeyed, and it felt like my hand was touching dry ice. She prophesied over him, and he started weeping and shaking like a little baby. Then she turned to me and said, "There was a generational curse of leukemia over him. He was already going into the beginning stages of it, but God has healed him."

Two men from our staff picked him up like a hunk of timber and loaded him into a station wagon to take him home. When he got there, the men laid him on the couch, still unconscious. His wife, recognizing the power of God, took their son who had a cold and laid him on Dave, and instantly the cold was gone.

Eunice left my office, and I have never seen her again to this day. But from the moment she prayed, my chest pains completely disappeared. You could see rubber marks around the church where I was running and jumping for joy! Dave came back the next day, and he, too, was amazed.

"I thought the woman was strange, but I feel like a new man," he said. I told him what she had said about leukemia, and he researched his family history and discovered that his grandfather and other relatives had died of leukemia.

But that day, the curse of leukemia was broken. Dave has been healthy and whole ever since, and so have I.

Healing Is For You!

I have always believed in healing, but rarely have I seen it happen in so dramatic a fashion as that day with Eunice. To say I was shocked and surprised would be putting it mildly. It isn't often you have someone dropping in who says God told her to travel across the country to pray for you and then identifies your exact condition!

But I knew that God was at work. Healing is the right of any Christian. Jesus paid for your healing when He accepted thirty-nine cruel stripes on His back at Pilate's whipping post. Some people don't believe that, but the evidence from the Gospels is simply overwhelming. Everywhere Jesus went, He left a trail of healed people in His wake. It was one of the pillars of His ministry.

And He still does it today. I and millions of other people can tell you it's true. Radical healing is for you, for me, and for everyone who asks.

The purpose of this book is to de-mystify the subject of healing and give you the faith to believe for your own healing or the healing of someone you love. This healing is available to you *right now*. It's a promise extended to you at this very moment. This book will help you reach out and take hold of it.

By the time you reach the last page, you will have the faith to believe for your own healing or the healing of someone you care about. You will understand what keeps people from being healed. You will also know what kinds of attitudes and actions bring about healing.

Many people sincerely believe in healing but have never experienced it. They live with physical ailments but can't seem to get free. Maybe you are one of them.

It's time to move from head knowledge to actual experience. It's time to start living in the promise of good health that Jesus bought for us. It's time to tell sickness, "Get out of my life! I will not tolerate you robbing me anymore." It's time to take God at His Word.

> Bless the LORD, O my soul, and forget not all his benefits: Who forgiveth all thine iniquities; *who healeth all thy diseases.*
>
> —Psalm 103:2-3 (KJV, italics added)

This book can be your prescription for God-given, Bible-promised, ever-enduring health! Let's get started on the pathway to *Radical Healing!*

*God has always been in
the miracle-working
business.*

Chapter One

How To Be Radically Healed

Joanie was a high-energy, fun-loving young lady until she was stricken with a mysterious back disease in her freshman year of high school. Doctors removed her tailbone, but the pain continued to spread. Gone was her active schedule and anything resembling a social life. Instead of going to basketball games and after-school events, she went to the hospital to be fitted for body casts and undergo treatments.

But things didn't get better. In the next twenty years, she underwent six surgeries and was treated by sixty different doctors who told her that three of her spinal disks were completely gone. Nothing helped. By the early 1990s, she was bedridden and would leave home only to see the doctors. During the day, she moved from the bed to the couch by way of a wheelchair, and even that caused severe pain.

She was, in her own words, a vegetable.

"Why would God let this happen?" she often wondered. "Haven't I served Him all my life?"

The doctors gave up hope of curing her and instead prescribed heavy doses of painkillers they said she would have to take for the rest of her life, but they only worsened Joanie's depression. She began to lose body functions and couldn't even write her own name.

Finally one night, after taking a dose of the prescription drugs, she felt compelled to go to church, as if something was drawing her to the sanctuary where she hadn't been in two years. She made her way there with the help of her husband and managed to stay awake despite the sedating effect of the drugs. When the altars opened, she overcame her discomfort of being in public and hobbled to the front where she poured out her heart and her tears to God.

Suddenly she felt a new sensation come over her: joy, peace, a tingling from head to toe. Not only did the physical pain dissipate, but her happiness burst forth like a spring of fresh water, and she knew that she had been healed. She turned to see her husband

and daughter, and they began to cry and hug like never before. Mom had been healed!

Three days later, Joanie went to her doctor's office and amazed him by walking in normally and upright. He put her through a variety of examinations and then wrote "Divine intervention" across the top of her chart (Pentecostal Evangel, September 15, 1996, pg. 29).

A Healing God

God has always been in the miracle-working business, doing for others what He did that night for Joanie. When I think of how Jesus healed people, I get so many images in my mind.

The woman pressing in to touch the hem of His garment ...

Blind Bartimaeus crying out from the side of the road outside Jericho ...

The ten lepers begging to be made clean ...

The little girl who was brought back to life ...

The paralyzed man lowered through the roof of a home ...

But one miracle always touches my heart, and from it we can learn the basic truths about this wonderful gift from God.

> Once more he visited Cana in Galilee, where He had turned the water into wine. And there was a certain royal official whose son lay sick at Capernaum.
>
> When this man heard that Jesus had arrived in Galilee from Judea, he went to him and begged him to come and heal his son, who was close to death.
>
> "Unless you people see miraculous signs and wonders," Jesus told him, "you will never believe."
>
> The royal official said, "Sir, come down before my child dies."
>
> Jesus replied, "You may go. Your son will live." The man took Jesus at his word and departed.
>
> While he was still on the way, his servants met him with the news that his boy was living.
>
> When he inquired as to the time when his son got better, they said to him, "The fever left him yesterday at the seventh hour."
>
> Then the father realized that this was the exact time at which Jesus had said to him, "Your son will live." So he and all his household believed.
>
> —John 4:46-53

There are eight principles embedded in this account that will help us understand and receive radical healing as did Joanie and the centurion's son.

❐ *Number One: Affliction can bring a person to Jesus.*

It's sad but true that many people never think about Jesus until tragedy strikes. Many professing

Christians wouldn't think of spending an hour in prayer — until they have a life-or-death need.

The centurion probably wouldn't have walked twenty-five miles to see Jesus if his son hadn't been sick. That's what it took for him to hunger after God, and it may be what it takes for you or someone you love.

If you are praying for a loved one to be released from a bad situation, keep in mind that perhaps God is using it to get their attention. Pray not just that the bad thing is removed but that it will bring them to Jesus.

There was a man named Brad who didn't believe in God and was obsessed with material possessions: luxury cars, fast boats, and fine jewelry. One day he found a lump under his collarbone. He had always suffered from back problems, sometimes so painful that he had to climb stairs on his hands and knees, but now the problems seemed to indicate something else. He went to the doctor who conducted a biopsy and discovered cancer, confirming Brad's worst fears. It was eating away his spine.

Within weeks his weight dropped from 170 to 132 pounds, and he began radiation treatment.

Brad was scared to the point of death. Indeed, he was on death's door when he began to think about God and all that he had heard about being born again. He didn't know Jesus, but when he prayed to God and reached out for stability, he experienced a revelation of Jesus that transformed his heart. Suddenly he understood what salvation meant, and he asked for forgiveness for his materialistic, God-ignoring life.

Whether he lived or died didn't matter to him anymore because God took away his fear of death. But God chose to heal Brad. The radiation treatments progressed amazingly well, he gained weight, and his strength returned. He was more humble than ever. Years and decades passed, and the cancer did not return. Brad grew strong in the Lord and became a mature believer (Pentacostal Evangel, August 11, 1996, pg. 29).

Did God cause the cancer? Never! But did He allow it to drive Brad to Him? In Brad's opinion, He did. If affliction comes into your life, let it push you closer to Him. Perhaps it's the prelude to divine healing!

❑   *Number Two: There is no distance in the power of faith.*

I remember a lady who was taken to the emergency room of a hospital in my city. She was dying of emphysema, and medics were trying to give her oxygen as she gasped for air. Her family of Spirit-filled believers called prayer partners and started a spiritual bombardment of Heaven for her health, and as they did a miracle took place. The dying woman said it was like a whirlwind came into the emergency room, and a breath from Heaven came into her mouth and down into her body, and she was able to breathe again. She left that hospital and lived a long and fruitful life, never bothered by emphysema again.

But nobody laid hands on her. Prayer was not made at her bedside but from miles away. That tells us there is no distance in the power of faith and prayer.

Jesus never met the centurion's son. As far as we know, they didn't look each other in the eye. Jesus didn't physically touch him, and yet the boy was healed.

Some people want to wait until they have a vision or a sign from above to summon their faith for healing. They want personal attention — a touch, a prayer with hands laid on their sick body. But it doesn't always happen that way.

If you have loved ones far away who are suffering, your prayers can be just as powerful as if you were holding their hand. Healing prayers can circle the globe without losing an ounce of effectiveness.

❐ *Number Three: We must believe without visible evidence.*

Imagine what kinds of thoughts this centurion must have had on the way home. The devil was probably right in his ear saying, "You walked all that way for nothing. Your son is probably dead by now. What kind of father are you, going twenty-five miles away when your son needed you? You're never going to see him again."

But he kept walking and believed the word of Jesus!

If you are waiting and believing for healing, the difficult time comes when there is no indication of the healing — when Jesus says, "Go, it has been done," but you see no proof of it. The lump remains. The sickness still clings to your lungs, or heart, or stomach.

Have you ever seen a court trial where the outcome hinged on a key piece of evidence? Having enough evidence can send a guilty person to jail or set an innocent person free.

What is the evidence we present in the Court of Healing? Faith! The more evidence — faith — we pile up, the more certain the outcome.

Faith is the "evidence of things not seen" — things that are real but invisible to us.

But to God, faith is fully visible.

> Now faith is the substance of things hoped for, the evidence of things not seen.
>
> —Hebrews 11:1 (KJV)

Faith became the centurion's evidence. He had nothing else to hold onto. He didn't need to see with his physical eyes because he believed in the invisible evidence laid out before him!

Christians should not need a steady diet of the spectacular to believe that God is doing something. God is trying to get us to be more mature. Jesus said in frustration:

> Unless you people see miraculous signs and wonders ... you will never believe.
>
> —John 4:48

He doesn't want us to rely on signs and wonders or things seen with our physical eyes. He wants us to let faith be our evidence. We should let faith rise up inside of us and say, "Thus saith the Lord: I shall live and not die!"

If you are believing for healing, you have two choices: Believe in the sickness or believe in the cure. The cure is Jesus and His promise that by His stripes we are healed.

> But he *was* wounded for our transgressions, *he was* bruised for our iniquities: the chastisement of our peace *was* upon him; and with his stripes we are healed.
>
> —Isaiah 53:5 (KJV)

> Who his own self bare our sins in his own body on the tree, that we, being dead to sins, should live unto righteousness: by whose stripes ye were healed.
>
> —1 Peter 2:24 (KJV)

Let that be your evidence!

❐ *Number Four: Faith always involves an action.*

In receiving healing from God, passive faith is dead faith. James 2:26 says:

> As the body without the spirit is dead, so faith without deeds is dead.

Faith is reaching out and laying hands on the sick. Faith is the sick person believing that the moment hands are laid on him, he is beginning to recover.

How do you take action? By doing something you couldn't do before. If you couldn't bend over and touch your toes; by faith, start bending over and touching your toes. There is only one way faith can be seen, and that is by doing. If you believe you are healed, begin to *act* like you're healed. *Talk* like you are healed. *Walk* like you are healed.

When Jesus told the centurion to go home, the man obeyed without saying, "Could you verify that for me?" He *acted*.

I recall reading about Smith Wigglesworth who would break people's crutches and canes and say, "Be healed in the Name of Jesus." The crippled were forced to act on their faith because their canes and crutches were in splinters! They would wobble around and even fall down; but before long, because of acting on the Word of God, they were running around the auditorium.

Let your body and mind act in accordance with your faith, and begin doing — not just believing.

In the next chapter, we'll look at more principles of healing from our text, John 4:46-53.

The moment you believe
God is the moment your
miracle is dispatched even
if it takes time for you to
see it come to pass.

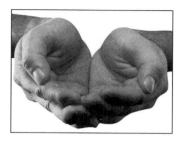

Chapter Two

How To Be Radically Healed, Part II

❏ *Number Five: The moment you really believe is when the healing comes.*

Meriel was terrified.

She knew cancer ran in her family, and all her life she had feared becoming another cancer-victim statistic. She had three lovely children and couldn't imagine them growing up without a mother.

But she had begun bleeding from her rectum after every bowel movement and not just slight bleeding but significant amounts of blood. The doctor performed several tests and discovered cancer not just in her rectum and colon but in her breast. The remedy: Remove the rectum and part of the colon. Meriel was devastated.

For weeks she didn't go to church and could hardly face her family. Then one day, as she lay on her bed praying, she heard a man's voice — not with her physical ears but in her heart: "We didn't have to make an abdominal cut. Everything is all right." The voice had a peculiar accent that Meriel had never heard before and was spoken with excitement. She pondered the experience but was still steeped in depression.

The next three nights as she slept, she heard the same words spoken by the same voice, and she grew more curious about what it meant. Before the surgery, her Bible study group anointed her with oil and prayed for her. The Lord sent a prophetic message that she would be healed.

"Could it be true?" she wondered. "And why do I keep hearing that voice with the strange accent?"

Meriel went in for surgery. She changed into a gown, laid on the gurney, and let the nurses start an IV in her arm. Then, as they wheeled her into the operating room, she heard a voice. It was her anesthesiologist speaking, but the accent was unmistakable: It was the voice God had given her during the night. She came out of surgery in half the expected time, and the surgeons reported that the cancer had not adhered to the rectal wall. Meaning, there was no need to make an abdominal cut or remove any part of her bowels.

Two weeks later, a mammography showed no mass in her breast.

God had given Meriel an "audio glimpse" into what would happen, and then He healed her completely!

What does this teach? That healing comes before we see it manifested.

> When he [the centurion] inquired as to the time when his son got better, they said to him, "The fever left him yesterday at the seventh hour."
>
> Then the father realized that this was the exact time at which Jesus had said to him, "Your son will live..."
>
> —John 4:52-53b [Brackets added]

Meriel heard the voice before she was healed, but in God's eyes, the healing was an accomplished fact before Meriel received it.

The moment you believe God is the moment your miracle is dispatched even if it takes time for you to see it come to pass.

❐ *Number Six: Healing doesn't happen the same way all the time.*

Jesus healed in a variety of ways. Sometimes He did it from a distance. Sometimes He laid hands on the sick. Sometimes He healed them before they died and sometimes after they were in the grave.

I have seen people healed when they were anointed with oil or during the worship time without anyone praying for them. I have known others who were healed at their homes, in their cars, and while at work.

Smith Wigglesworth wouldn't just pray for people — he attacked their sickness physically, sometimes punching people in the stomach and sending them flying across the room. If the people hadn't been healed, he might have received a lot more criticism!

One time Jesus spat on the ground, made mud with His saliva, and rubbed it on the eyes of a blind man (John 9:6)! Sometimes He gave a command to drive the sickness out; sometimes He told people to go to the temple, and their healing would happen there.

There are principles to how healing works, but there is no single formula. God can use any method He chooses. Be open to the creative way He wants to heal you!

❐ *Number Seven (I like this one!): Faith is contagious.*

...So he and all his household believed.

—John 4:53c

The faith of the centurion led to the salvation of his whole family! This happens all the time in churches across America. The faith of a father frequently leads to the conversion of an entire family.

Remember the jailer from Philippi in the book of Acts? He and his whole household believed after he experienced a miracle.

When you are healed, your faith will spill over to unsaved loved ones. You will have an opportunity to share at family gatherings or over the backyard fence about what God did for you, and the proof will be irrefutable. Your situation will be a sign and wonder for people, causing them to think on the things of God and come to salvation.

Your healing will become contagious!

❒ *Number Eight: God heals for a purpose.*

There was a man named Ko Chong Yuan who was a parachutist with an elite military airborne company in Taiwan. He would leap from a plane at ten thousand feet as part of his training.

One day, as he plummeted toward the earth, his parachute malfunctioned, and Ko Chong slammed into the ground breaking many bones and injuring his brain. It was a miracle that he lived. For two years he was unable to stand, and he fell into despair. Then an evangelist came to town to hold a crusade, and the Holy Spirit worked marvelously, healing people in every service. Ko Chong's family, encouraged by the reports, brought him to a service to receive prayer.

The evangelist stood in front of him, and two of Ko Chong's soldier friends lifted him out of his chair causing his legs to dangle uselessly. The evangelist sensed that God was about to perform a dramatic miracle, so he asked, "Do you know that God is going to heal you?" Ko Chong replied, "Yes, I believe it!" Before the evangelist could lay a hand on him, the power of God came upon him; he flung off his friends' arms and began to walk down the aisle.

But the story doesn't end there. Not only was he saved, healed, and baptized in the Holy Spirit; Ko Chong quit his military career and became a pastor of a church and was responsible for leading thousands of people to Christ, including some in mainland China (Pentacostal Evangel, January 14, 1996, pg. 20).

Many times when Jesus healed someone they immediately latched onto a purpose. When Jesus came to Peter's house, He saw Peter's mother-in-law sick with a fever. He touched her hand, the fever left her, and she got up and began to wait on them. She immediately became a servant. She used the energy and wholeness God gave her to wait on the King of kings.

After Jesus healed the demonized man in the tombs of the Gadarenes, he begged to follow Jesus. But He told him to go into his village and tell everyone what God had done for him. He enlisted him as a preacher! (Luke 8:26-39)

Maybe you want to be healed, so you can walk again. Or go outside. Or work full-time without a great deal of pain. Or pick up your grandchild.

Jesus wants these things for you too. But He also has a larger purpose for you — to turn you into a servant and preacher of the Gospel! I'm certain that the centurion told everyone he knew about Jesus after his son was healed. I can't imagine him sitting on the information!

What does God have for you to do? What purpose is on the other side of your healing? God intends your healing to be for His glory in a way you can't fully imagine. Be open and available to new ways of service for Him after He heals you.

Let's summarize the principles we've learned in the last two chapters, so we can build our faith:

1. Affliction can bring a person to Jesus.

2. There is no distance in the power of faith.

3. We must believe without visible evidence.

4. Faith always involves an action.

5. The moment you really believe is when the healing comes.

6. Healing doesn't happen the same way all the time.

7. Faith is contagious!

8. God heals for a purpose.

Next we'll look at three of the main things that cause people to be sick.

Chapter Three

What Causes Sickness?

Death was swift and horrible during the bubonic plague in 1350 AD. First, small blisters would appear on a person's arms and legs, and their skin would turn dark gray (giving rise to the term "the Black Death"). Then the lymph nodes in the neck, armpits, and groin would swell, and they would vomit blood relentlessly for three or four days; by which time the lymph nodes would burst, and they would die suddenly, sometimes while standing. One observer said victims often "ate lunch with their friends and ate dinner with their ancestors in paradise."

The plague came on suddenly, spread by fleas and rats, and killed one-third of the people in Europe in the space of three years. That's the same as if 100 million Americans were to die between presidential elections. The plague was so contagious that families expelled children who showed signs of sickness.

Corpses lay forsaken in the houses with their valuables, gold, and jewels untouched. Servants were paid a high price to bring the bodies out, but no priest would come near them, so they were dumped in massive ditches outside the cities.

We can't imagine that kind of misery today because vaccines and antibiotics have wiped out many of the most-feared diseases. Thank God that science has exposed the nasty little germs and viruses that have caused so much pain. But the Bible also warns of three specific causes of sickness that are spiritual in nature, and we should guard against them as if *they* were the plague.

Sin

> And it came to pass on a certain day, as he was teaching, that there were Pharisees and doctors of the law sitting by, which were come out of every town of Galilee, and Judaea, and Jerusalem: and the power of the Lord was *present* to heal them.
>
> And, behold, men brought in a bed a man which was taken with a palsy: and they sought means to bring him in, and to lay *him* before Him.
>
> And when they could not find by what *way* they might bring him in because of the multitude, they went upon the housetop, and let him down through the tiling with his couch into the midst before Jesus.
>
> And when he saw their faith, he said unto him, "Man, thy sins are forgiven thee."

> And the scribes and the Pharisees began to reason, saying, Who is this which speaketh blasphemies? Who can forgive sins, but God alone?
>
> But when Jesus perceived their thoughts, he answering said unto them, "What reason ye in your hearts?
>
> Whether is easier, to say, Thy sins be forgiven thee; or to say, Rise up and walk?
>
> But that ye may know that the Son of man hath power upon earth to forgive sins, (he said unto the sick of the palsy,) I say unto thee, Arise, and take up thy couch, and go into thy house."
>
> And immediately he rose up before them, and took up that whereon he lay, and depared to his own house, glorifying God.
>
> And thy were all amazed, and they glorified God, and were filled with fear, saying, We have seen strange things to day.
>
> —Luke 5:17-26 (KJV)

Sin is linked to sickness in a number of places in both the Old and New Testaments. Once when Jesus was preaching in a house, some men lowered a paralytic through the roof. Jesus saw their faith, He said:

> "Friend, your sins are forgiven."
>
> —Luke 5:20

This was the first time Jesus linked sin and sickness. What is the connection? Sin causes guilt and shame which makes it difficult for the human spirit to reach out to God. We feel unworthy of being well.

James, the brother of Jesus, wrote in his letter:

> Is any one of you sick? He should call the elders of the church to pray over him and anoint him with oil in the name of the Lord. And the prayer offered in faith will make the sick person well; the Lord will raise him up. If he has sinned, he will be forgiven.
>
> Therefore confess your sins to each other and pray for each other so that you may be healed.
>
> —James 5:14-16a

This passage links healing, confession, and forgiveness.

Have you ever held a sin inside of you, bottled up? After a while, didn't it start eating at you? When I hold onto an unconfessed sin, I start to feel sick — until I confess it and ask forgiveness.

Now imagine that happening over a longer period of time. It's no wonder that sin causes disease!

I have known many people who decided to live outside of God's will and suffered and died prematurely from illnesses. The human body was meant to live in harmony with God. Sin throws the mind, body, and spirit out of whack.

We can't dismiss the fact that sickness is sometimes an outward symbol of the curse on our lives that comes when we disobey God's commands. In Deuteronomy 28:15-68, God enumerated the sicknesses that would afflict the children of Israel if they abandoned His commandments. The list included:

- the plague

- severe burning fever

- inflammation

- boils from head to foot

- tumors

- scabs

- the itch that cannot be healed

- madness

- blindness

- confusion of heart

- serious and prolonged sickness

- every other illness known to man

I have no doubt that some sickness afflicts people today because they reject the Lord.

> And it shall come to pass, if thou shalt hearken diligently unto the voice of the LORD thy God, to observe *and* to do all his commandments which I command thee this day, that the LORD thy God will set thee on high above all nations of the earth:

And all these blessings shall come on thee, and overtake thee, if thou shalt hearken unto the voice of the LORD thy God.

Blessed *shalt* thou *be* in the city, and blessed *shalt* thou *be* in the field.

Blessed *shall be* the fruit of thy body, and the fruit of thy ground, and the fruit of thy cattle, the increase of thy kine, and the flocks of thy sheep.

Blessed *shall be* thy basket and thy store.

Blessed *shalt* thou *be* when thou comest in, and blessed *shalt* thou *be* when thou goest out.

The LORD shall cause thine enemies that rise up against thee to be smitten before thy face: they shall come out against thee one way, and flee before thee seven ways.

The LORD shall command the blessing upon thee in thy storehouses, and in all that thou settest thine hand unto; and he shall bless thee in the land which the LORD thy God giveth thee.

The LORD shall establish thee an holy people unto himself, as he hath sworn unto thee, if thou shalt keep the commandments of the LORD thy God, and walk in his ways.

And all people of the earth shall see that thou art called by the name of the LORD; and they shall be afraid of thee.

And the LORD shall make thee plenteous in goods, in the fruit of thy body, and in the fruit of thy cattle, and in the fruit of thy ground, in the land which the LORD sware unto thy fathers to give thee.

The LORD shall open unto thee his good treasure, the heaven to give the rain unto thy land in his season, and to bless all the work of thine hand: and thou shalt lend unto many nations, and thou shalt not borrow.

And the LORD shall make thee the head, and not the tail; and thou shalt be above only, and thou shalt not be beneath; if that thou hearken unto the commandments of the LORD thy God, which I command thee this day, to observe and to do *them*.

And thou shalt not go aside from any of the words which I command thee this day, *to* the right hand, or *to* the left, to go after other gods to serve them.

But it shall come to pass, if thou wilt not hearken unto the voice of the LORD thy God, to observe to do all his commandments and his statutes which I command thee this day; that all these curses shall come upon thee, and overtake thee:

Cursed *shalt* thou *be* in the city, and cursed *shalt* thou *be* in the field.

Cursed *shall be* thy basket and thy store.

Cursed *shall be* the fruit of thy body, and the fruit of thy land, the increase of thy kine, and the flocks of thy sheep.

Cursed *shalt* thou *be* when thou comest in, and cursed *shalt* thou *be* when thou goest out.

The LORD shall send upon thee cursing, vexation, and rebuke, in all that thou settest thine hand unto for to do, until thou be destroyed, and until thou perish quickly; because of the wickedness of thy doings, whereby thou hast forsaken me.

The LORD shall make the pestilence cleave unto thee, until he have consumed thee from off the land, whither thou goest to possess it.

The LORD shall smite thee with a consumption, and with a fever, and with an inflammation, and with an extreme burning, and with the sword, and with blasting, and with mildew; and they shall pursue thee until thou perish.

And thy heaven that *is* over thy head shall be brass, and the earth that is under thee *shall be* iron.

The LORD shall make the rain of thy land powder and dust: from heaven shall it come down upon thee, until thou be destroyed.

The LORD shall cause thee to be smitten before thine enemies: thou shalt go out one way against them, and flee seven ways before them: and shalt be removed into all the kingdoms of the earth.

And thy carcase shall be meat unto all fowls of the air, and unto the beasts of the earth, and no man shall fray *them* away.

The LORD will smite thee with the botch of Egypt, and with the emerods, and with the scab, and with the itch, whereof thou canst not be healed.

The LORD shall smite thee with madness, and blindness, and astonishment of heart:

And thou shalt grope at noonday, as the blind gropeth in darkness, and thou shalt not prosper in thy ways: and thou shalt be only oppressed and spoiled evermore, and no man shall save *thee.*

Thou shalt betroth a wife, and another man shall lie with her: thou shalt build an house, and thou shalt not dwell therein: thou shalt plant a vineyard, and shalt not gather the grapes thereof.

Thine ox *shall be* slain before thine eyes, and thou shalt not eat thereof: thine ass *shall be* violently taken away from before thy face, and shall not be restored to thee: thy sheep *shall be* given unto thine enemies, and thou shalt have none to rescue *them*.

Thy sons and thy daughters *shall be* given unto another people, and thine eyes shall look, and fail *with longing* for them all the day long: and *there shall be* no might in thine hand.

The fruit of thy land, and all thy labours, shall a nation which thou knowest not eat up; and thou shalt be only oppressed and crushed alway:

So that thou shalt be mad for the sight of thine eyes which thou shalt see.

The LORD shall smite thee in the knees, and in the legs, with a sore botch that cannot be healed, from the sole of thy foot unto the top of thy head.

The LORD shall bring thee, and thy king which thou shalt set over thee, unto a nation which neither thou nor thy fathers have known; and there shalt thou serve other gods, wood and stone.

And thou shalt become an astonishment, a proverb, and a byword, among all nations whither the LORD shall lead thee.

Thou shalt carry much seed out into the field, and shalt gather *but* little in; for the locust shall consume it.

Thou shalt plant vineyards, and dress *them*, but shalt neither drink *of* the wine, nor gather *the grapes*; for the worms shall eat them.

Thou shalt have olive trees throughout all thy coasts, but thou shalt not anoint *thyself* with the oil; for thine olive shall cast *his fruit*.

> Thou shalt beget sons and daughters, but thou shalt not enjoy them; for they shall go into captivity.
>
> All thy trees and fruit of thy land shall the locust consume.
>
> The stranger that *is* within thee shall get up above thee very high; and thou shalt come down very low.
>
> He shall lend to thee, and thou shalt not lend to him: he shall be the head, and thou shalt be the tail.
>
> Moreover all these curses shall come upon thee, and shall pursue thee, and overtake thee, till thou be destroyed; because thou hearkenedst not unto the voice of the LORD thy God, to keep his commandments and his statutes which he commanded thee:
>
> And they shall be upon thee for a sign and for a wonder, and upon thy seed for ever.
>
> Because thou servedst not the LORD thy God with joyfulness, and with gladness of heart, for the abundance of all *things*;
>
> Therefore shalt thou serve thine enemies which the LORD shall send against thee, in hunger, and in thirst, and in nakedness, and in want of all *things*: and he shall put a yoke of iron upon thy neck, until he have destroyed thee.
>
> —Deuteronomy 28:1-48 (KJV)

For maximum health, examine your spiritual life. See if there is any unresolved sin. Look for tender spots in your spirit that you would rather keep hidden from others. By confessing those things and grabbing onto God's wonderful forgiveness through Jesus Christ, you can get rid of sin.

Unbelief

Some Christians are sick because they don't believe God can heal them. Their human reasoning and logical calculation get in the way. When Jesus forgave the paralytic, the Gospel says:

> Now some teachers of the law were sitting there, thinking to themselves, "Why does this fellow talk like that? He's blaspheming! Who can forgive sins but God alone?" Immediately Jesus knew in his spirit that this was what they were thinking in their hearts, and he said to them, "Why are you thinking these things?
>
> —Mark 2:6-8

When you begin to weigh the logic of something God has said rather than accepting it in faith, it leads to doubt. It's like demanding evidence that can be seen rather than accepting the unseen evidence. You can build a wall that separates you from the power of God.

Sometimes your unbelief literally speaks louder than words! Jesus knew what the teachers were thinking that day though they didn't say it out loud. There is a gift of the Holy Spirit called the word of knowledge that is available to us even today under the direction of the Holy Spirit.

One Sunday morning, when I was preaching, I began to perceive people's thoughts. It has only happened to me one time, and it was one of the eeriest experiences I've ever had. As I was preaching, I could look at a person and know what he or she was thinking.

One man was sitting in the pew, and I perceived his critical thoughts. He was mentally bad-mouthing the sermon, the church, and even the Lord, and it hung over him like a stench. The Lord said to me, "His time is short. Call him to Me." I walked over to him and said, "Sir, I don't know you, but would you like to receive Jesus as your Lord? He loves you; He died for you. Please accept salvation." The man started swearing at me! I walked away not knowing what else to do.

The service ended, and I stopped being able to know people's thoughts, which was just as well because it takes a lot of grace to *not* respond to them! Not long afterward, I got a call from a funeral home asking me to perform a funeral. I went over to view the body, and there in the casket was that man who had sworn at me. Only God knows if he died in his unbelief.

I had a similar experience on another occasion. There was a couple in the church who seemed talented, but for some reason we never felt like we could put them in a position of leadership. I couldn't understand why because they were nice enough people, but something in my spirit said not to elevate them yet.

One Sunday afternoon I was praying in my office, and suddenly the Lord allowed me to supernaturally eavesdrop on the couple. Not only was I perceiving their thoughts, I was hearing their words from a distance. They were driving to lunch after church, and it was as if I was in the back seat of their car listening to everything they said. I heard them criticizing me and another pastor saying that the reason their ministry was not taking off was because I didn't recognize talent when I saw it.

Then the experience ended, and I was back in my office. It was as though I had fallen asleep and had a dream, and yet it was so real.

I didn't say anything about it all week, but the next Sunday morning I thought I would test it. I stood in the pulpit and said, "There's a couple in the church who can't seem to break into leadership. Last week I had an unusual experience after the service. It was as if I was riding in the back seat of their car, and I heard them criticizing me and another pastor."

I repeated the exact words I had heard, and after the service I headed for the back room, and there was the man who had spoken the words. He was not with his wife. I shook hands with him, and his face was red and sweaty. Veins were bulging out of his neck. "I was doing all right until I came to church today!" he said. He had been chastened by a word of knowledge from the Lord.

Sometimes we need that kind of jarring experience to jolt us out of unbelief. But on the day Jesus healed the paralytic, not even a word of knowledge could pry the teachers of the law from their critical thinking. The story starts by saying that the power of the Lord was present to heal that day — and that included the teachers of the law. Had they overcome their unbelief, they could have received a miracle.

> ...And the power of the Lord was present for him to heal the sick.
>
> —Luke 5:17c

But there is no record that they ever received healing from Jesus. The power was there, but unbelief stood in their way.

How about you? Does an unbelieving attitude get in the way of receiving your healing? Are you critical of the reality of divine healing in your heart? Do you try to make sense of God's ways with your mind rather than receiving it by faith with your spirit?

If so, you are putting up a wall against a healing miracle. Forcefully shake loose those old thoughts of unbelief — don't spare even one of them. The Bible is clear: You must believe to receive.

> Now FAITH is being sure of what we hope for and certain of what we do not see.
>
> —Hebrew 11:1 (Emphasis Added)

> And without FAITH it is impossible to please God, because anyone who comes to him must believe that he exists and that he rewards those who earnestly seek him.
>
> —Hebrew 11:6 (Emphasis Added)

> "'If you can'?" said Jesus. "Everything is possible for him who BELIEVES."
>
> —Mark 9:23 (Emphasis Added)

> Just then a woman who had been subject to bleeding for twelve years came up behind him and touched the edge of his cloak.
>
> She said to herself, "If I only touch his cloak, I will be healed."
>
> Jesus turned and saw her. "Take heart, daughter," he said, "YOUR FAITH HAS HEALED YOU." And the woman was healed from that moment.
>
> —Matthew 9:20-22 (Emphasis Added)

> As Jesus went on from there, two blind men followed him, calling out, "Have mercy on us, Son of David!"
>
> When he had gone indoors, the blind men came to him, and he asked them, "Do you believe that I am able to do this?" "Yes, Lord," they replied.

Then he touched their eyes and said, "ACCORD-
ING TO YOUR FAITH WILL IT BE DONE TO
YOU"; and their sight was restored.

—Matthew 9:27-30a (Emphasis Added)

Then they came to Jericho. As Jesus and his disciples, together with a large crowd, were leaving the city, a blind man, Bartimaeus (that is, the
Son of Timaeus), was sitting by the roadside
begging.

When he heard that it was Jesus of Nazareth, he
began to shout, "Jesus, Son of David, have mercy
on me!"

Many rebuked him and told him to be quiet,
but he shouted all the more, "Son of David, have
mercy on me!"

Jesus stopped and said, "Call him." So they
called to the blind man, "Cheer up! On your feet!
He's calling you."

Throwing his cloak aside, he jumped to his feet
and came to Jesus.

"What do you want me to do for you?" Jesus
asked him. The blind man said, "Rabbi, I want
to see."

"Go," said Jesus, "YOUR FAITH HAS HEALED
YOU." Immediately he received his sight and
followed Jesus along the road.

—Mark 10:46-52 (Emphasis Added)

He replied, "If you have FAITH as small as a
mustard seed, you can say to this mulberry tree,
'Be uprooted and planted in the sea,' and it will
obey you."

—Luke 17:6 (Emphasis Added)

> In Lystra there sat a man crippled in his feet, who was lame from birth and had never walked.
>
> He listened to Paul as he was speaking. Paul looked directly at him, saw that he had FAITH TO BE HEALED and called out, "Stand up on your feet!" At that, the man jumped up and began to walk.
>
> —Acts 14:8-10 (Emphasis Added)

Start believing, exercise faith, and watch the power of God flow to you!

In the next chapter, we'll discuss one final, supernatural cause of sickness.

Most doctors would never tell a patient that his problem was spiritual in nature.

Chapter Four

Demons And Sickness

Picture this: A man goes to the doctor because he's been feeling under the weather for a few months and can't seem to shake it. He sits on the examination table, and the doctor begins to check him out — putting a stethoscope to his chest and back; looking in his ears, eyes, and throat. Finally, the doctor steps back with a sigh and puts his hands in his white coat.

"I can't see any physical reason for you to be feeling sick," he says. "Your membranes are healthy. Your heart and lungs are working normally. Your blood tests came back normal. But I think I know what you suffer from."

"What?" the man says eagerly.

"Demons," says the doctor.

The idea of a doctor telling the man that demons are making him sick sounds comical, and that is partly the point. Most doctors would never tell a patient that his problem was spiritual in nature. It strikes the modern mind as hocus-pocus from an uncivilized time. But have we ruled out the real cause of some afflictions?

Jesus, the Great Physician, was able to see which diseases were caused by demons and which were physical, and He wasn't afraid to call it like it was. One day He was a guest speaker in a synagogue, and:

> ... a woman was there who had been crippled by a spirit for eighteen years. She was bent over and could not straighten up at all.
>
> —Luke 13:11

Her spine was so curved that she was bowed over, grossly deformed. She had to walk with her head down around her waist if she could walk at all. She probably faced the ridicule that the disabled often face from heartless people, particularly in that culture where illness was considered a sign of God's judgment.

But Jesus wasn't afraid, and He didn't judge her. He identified it as a spirit of infirmity — a demon — and when He set her free from the demon, she was able to stand up straight.

> On a Sabbath Jesus was teaching in one of the synagogues, and a woman was there who had been crippled by a spirit for eighteen years. She was bent over and could not straighten up at all.
>
> When Jesus saw her, he called her forward and said to her, "Woman, you are set free from your infirmity."
>
> Then he put his hands on her, and immediately she straightened up and praised God.
>
> Indignant because Jesus had healed on the Sabbath, the synagogue ruler said to the people, "There are six days for work. So come and be healed on those days, not on the Sabbath."
>
> The Lord answered him, "You hypocrites! Doesn't each of you on the Sabbath untie his ox or donkey from the stall and lead it out to give it water?
>
> Then should not this woman, a daughter of Abraham, whom Satan has kept bound for eighteen long years, be set free on the Sabbath day from what bound her?"
>
> When he said this, all his opponents were humiliated, but the people were delighted with all the wonderful things he was doing.
>
> —Luke 13:10-17

What doctor would be so brave as to cast a demon out of an afflicted patient?

Another time Jesus encountered a man who was demon-possessed and couldn't talk.

> And when the demon was driven out, the man who had been mute spoke. The crowd was

> amazed and said, "Nothing like this has ever
> been seen in Israel."
>
> —Matthew 9:33

Demons try to tie up and render people ineffective. They are thieves of purpose. They want us to be mute, so we can't share the Gospel. They want us to be bent over, so we can't declare the glory of God with uplifted hands. There is no question that some people in our day are sick because of demons.

What is the solution? To deliver people from demonic control!

Send The Demons Fleeing

When I first became a pastor, I met a man who was too weak to accept Jesus. It happened after a Sunday evening service when my wife, Mary Jo, and I were locking up the church. There sat a man in the sanctuary who didn't appear to want to leave. I sat next to him and said, "You really need to accept Jesus." He said, "I know, but I can't. I don't know why." He seemed drained of energy, pale, and defeated. I put my hand on his head and said, "Thou foul spirit, in the Name of Jesus and by His shed blood, come out of this man!"

Suddenly, he let loose with blood-curdling screams. It was a horrible, gurgling sound, but it lasted only a moment. When he was quiet, I said,

"Now will you accept Jesus?" He looked so relieved, as if a straitjacket had been removed, and said, "Yes," and we prayed the prayer of salvation. He received Christ, went home, and got rid of all his satanic rock and roll music, drugs, and paraphernalia, and became a born-again, Spirit-filled Christian! He is a member of our church to this day.

In 1986 a minister named Johannes, president of an international prayer group, went to the then Soviet Union with a team of intercessors and boldly proclaimed that judgment was upon the god of the Soviet Union. Immediately afterward, he became tired, weak, and had pains in his chest. Doctors diagnosed him with heart disease.

He went into a state of depression for three years thinking his ministry was over, and he even had thoughts of suicide.

A Christian brother came to him and said, "I think a demon attached itself to you when you were in the Soviet Union. Would you like me to pray for deliverance for you?" Johannes readily agreed, and within thirty seconds, the physical problems were entirely gone.

> For our struggle is not against flesh and blood,
> but against the rulers, against the authorities,
> against the powers of this dark world and against

the spiritual forces of evil in the heavenly realms.

—Ephesians 6:12

Spiritual Infirmity

I wouldn't venture to guess how much illness is caused by demons, but I do think it's much more than most Christians think. What are the signs?

• The illness has no explanation.

• It's persistent and keeps coming back.

• The afflicted person has exposed himself to demonic attack through the occult, music inspired by demons, or spiritual warfare.

• Someone discerns the demonic origins through revelation from God.

Years ago I heard a Christian psychiatrist speak as part of a ministerial round table. He practiced in New York City and had been a Christian for many years but only received the baptism in the Holy Spirit three years prior. Before receiving the baptism in the Holy Spirit, he did not believe demons were real, but after receiving this deeper experience with the Holy Spirit, he began to recognize their work in some of his patients.

A young patient he had worked with for several years did not talk. You could talk to him, and he would smile and be friendly, but he would not say a word. He had talked before, but for some reason he suddenly quit. They psychoanalyzed and counseled him with no success.

Then this psychiatrist decided he was going to try a spiritual approach.

He put his hands on the man's head and said, "I adjure this spirit to come out of you in the Name of Jesus." Then he prayed in tongues. He did that every day for thirty days. Finally the young man spoke and was released from psychiatric care. The breakthrough came when somebody attacked the real problem.

Maybe you can't seem to focus, or your mind is weak in a certain area. Perhaps you have a debilitating illness that keeps you from leading a vibrant life.

Have you considered that it might be an attack of the devil? I encourage you to visit with your spirit-filled pastor or church leader and get prayer. Your healing might come surprisingly fast.

Demons can be troublesome, but they are not the most potent or powerful reason people stay sick. That comes from a source much closer to home.

*Sickness should never be
a way of life for a
Christian.*

Chapter Five

Why Some Stay Sick

Jim was working on his motorcycle on the patio one day, fixing it up and racing the engine when somehow it slipped into gear. Jim, still holding the handlebars, was dragged through a glass patio door and dumped on the living room floor with the motorcycle. His wife, hearing the crash, ran into the dining room and found him laying on the floor, cut and bleeding. She phoned for an ambulance.

After the ambulance arrived and took Jim to the hospital, she hoisted the motorcycle up and pushed it outside. Seeing that gas had spilled on the floor, she blotted it up with paper towels and threw them in the toilet.

Jim's injuries weren't serious, so he was treated and released. Back at the house, he looked at the shattered patio door and the damaged motorcycle. He felt so bad that he went into the bathroom, sat on the toilet, and smoked a cigarette. After finishing the cigarette, he flipped it between his legs into the toilet bowl — with the gasoline-soaked paper towels.

His wife heard the explosion downstairs and found Jim laying on the floor, his pants blown off, and with burns on his backside. She again phoned for the ambulance, and the same paramedics came to the house and loaded Jim onto the stretcher. While they were going down the steep stairs to the street, one of the paramedics asked her how Jim had burned himself. When she told him, he laughed so hard that the stretcher tipped over and dumped Jim down the rest of the steps, breaking his ankle.

Talk about a losing streak!

Some people, like Jim, have occasional bad days. Others seem to relish their reputation for suffering. All of us are acquainted with at least one person who is "Eeyore" in human form. You know Eeyore: the down-in-the-mouth donkey from the Winnie the Pooh books. No matter how good the news, he can find a gray lining in it.

Some people act like Eeyore all day, dragging themselves to work, to school, back home, complaining about this and that, always seeing the downside.

Even the church has its Eeyores, but they try to justify themselves.

"I suffer so much," they say. "I must be a modern-day Job."

Never mind that Job only suffered for nine months, and then God doubled the family and riches he had before. If someone says he is a modern-day Job, he should expect to be free from his afflictions in nine months!

But these people want to stay in their sickness—partly because they believe it's God's will for them to suffer or they think their sickness somehow brings glory to God.

What a mistake! Sickness should never be a way of life for a Christian. The apostle Peter wrote:

> He himself bore our sins in his body on the tree, so that we might die to sins and live for righteousness; by his wounds you have been healed.
>
> —1 Peter 2:24

Jesus purchased healing for us on the Cross. He no more wants us to live in sickness than He wants us to live in sin. Those things are past! Paul said our light affliction "is but for a moment" (2 Corinthians 4:17 KJV).

We must let go of this ungodly idea that sickness brings glory to God!

No Glory In Sickness

From a young age, kids learn to get attention by glorifying their sickness. They always want to show you their cut, bruise, or scrape. Sometimes they like the sympathy or the hugs they get. They may even trick their mom into letting them stay home from school because they don't feel well.

This mentality persists into adulthood. How many times do you ask someone how they're doing and they reply, "Not very well. My leg is acting up again." Sometimes the only news people have is which part of their body is causing trouble!

At the altars during prayer time at our church, I sometimes hear people telling a prayer minister about the physical problem they want prayer for. It's good to share what the problem is, so we can pray specifically for it, but after a while, you notice the same people week after week who come forward for prayer. They don't really want prayer as much as they want to gain your sympathy. They try to be the last in the healing line, so they can have a long conversation about their sickness. They don't take the wisdom of the Bible that says:

> ... the tongue of the wise is health.
>
> —**Proverbs 12:18b (KJV)**

In other words, the wise person speaks about health not sickness.

Good Suffering vs. Bad Suffering

Some suffering is good and legitimate. Some is bad and illegitimate. The apostle Peter wrote:

> Dear friends, do not be surprised at the painful trial you are suffering, as though something strange were happening to you. But rejoice that you participate in the sufferings of Christ, so that you may be overjoyed when his glory is revealed.
>
> —1 Peter 4:12-13

He was writing about persecution not sickness or disease!

Legitimate suffering is when we are criticized for righteousness' sake, persecuted, facing temptation, or being corrected by God. The Bible promises that we will be criticized. Jesus said that if they hated Him, they would hate us too. If you are being persecuted because of your godliness, the Bible says that is par for the course.

But sickness and disease never bring glory to us or to God.

You see, people misunderstand at what point Jesus is our example and at what point He is our substitute.

Jesus died on the Cross to be the substitute for the penalty of sin. Nobody ever has to die on the Cross again. We are not to follow Him in capital punishment. Only a fool would say, "I'm going to hang myself on a cross because that's what Jesus did."

On the Cross, He was our substitute for sin, sickness, and poverty. Those things are curses that we no longer have to live under.

In other things, Jesus was our example. We are to follow His example as best as we can, and that will inevitably include persecution for righteousness' sake.

But let's not confuse the suffering that comes from following His example with the illegitimate suffering from which He has redeemed us.

I have heard preachers say things such as, "Sister So-and-so is going through a serious trial. She has been sick for fourteen years, but this sickness has led her to a deeper relationship with God. She prays harder than she has ever prayed. She is so much more godly because of this sickness."

That preacher is in error. God never calls you to suffer sickness to draw closer to Him.

One time I asked an older gentleman how his wife was doing, and he said, "Not well at all. She's losing her memory. I want her to be healed, but it's up to God; if this is the way God wants it to be, we have to accept it."

I felt like telling him, "God's will toward healing your wife is settled. Jesus Christ was our substitute in sickness and disease. She can be healed today!"

Inviting The Wrong Suffering

Some Christians voluntarily give themselves over to sickness because they think they are due for something bad to happen. American believers feel guilty that there is not much persecution — no public beatings, stonings, or crucifixions of Christians — so they imagine that illness is God's way of giving us a dose of hard times. They completely change the meaning of these Scriptures on suffering.

There is no place where we are authorized to suffer sickness.

> But he *was* wounded for our transgressions, *he was* bruised for our iniquities: the chastisement of our peace *was* upon him; and with his stripes we are healed.
>
> —Isaiah 53:5 (KJV)
>
> ...He took up our infirmities and carried our diseases.
>
> —Matthew 8:17c

I'm not saying that Christians will never get sick. I am saying God's highest ideal is that we always live in good health. That's what we should shoot for. If I get 80 or 90 percent of the way there, I'm going to be a whole lot further than the people who shoot for nothing!

God has ordained that we live long, healthy lives. He wants you out of sickness and disease. Don't believe the lie that being sick brings glory to God.

Now let's look at other ways people become sickness magnets.

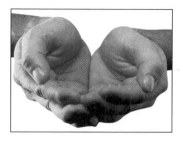

Chapter Six

How People Become Sickness Magnets

Before these days of pills and shots, people tried all sorts of remedies to get rid of sickness. During the plagues, they thought disease and death were transmitted by the strong odor of death that they smelled, so they burned aromatic leaves and herbs as protection.

Many believed that sound would drive the plague away, so towns rang church bells and fired cannons.

Some thought the disease was caused by the earth releasing poisonous vapors. Others said it was because people slept during the daytime, bathed, or ate olive oil.

One wise man said the remedy was to think about beautiful landscapes, gold, and precious stones and listen to melodious songs which would cheer the heart.

The Pope decided he would sit between two fires and breathe the pure air, which proved to be effective, since the germ that caused the plague was destroyed by heat.

Most people died during those days because they lacked the right kind of knowledge. One way to become a magnet for sickness is to stay ignorant of what causes it. Hosea 4:6a (KJV) says:

> **My people are destroyed from lack of knowledge.**

Let me share with you some of the ways people become "sickness magnets."

❐ *Number One: Ignorance of God's Word*

The Holy Spirit tries to always lead us into the right area of knowledge, including knowledge of cleanliness and how to avoid diseases, but we suffer needlessly when our ears are not tuned to Him. Many illnesses are caused by lack of knowledge, either on our part or the doctor's.

There are two ways to lack knowledge. First is to be ignorant of medical remedies that could help you. For centuries people suffered headaches and pains because nobody knew about aspirin or other painkillers. They also suffered horribly in surgery until someone discovered ether.

Now that we understand these substances, we can ease people's pain.

The second and more serious way to lack knowledge is by being ignorant of what the Bible says. Some Christians simply don't understand the promises the Bible makes about health.

There was a lady who played in our church orchestra. She was having trouble because she itched all over. I told her that I had been reading in Deuteronomy that the itch was under the curse of the law, and according to Galatians 3:13, Jesus redeemed us from the curse of the law. She immediately said, "Jesus redeemed me from the curse of the law, and the itch is under the curse of the law. This itch is illegitimate suffering." Before that service was over, she was jumping around, smiling from ear to ear. "The itch is gone," she said. She didn't even know what had caused it in the first place.

Another man I knew had a cold and wasn't sure it was God's will to heal him. I showed him the biblical basis for healing, and he prayed, "In Galatians 3:13, Jesus Christ redeemed me from the curse of the law. Therefore, I don't have to put up with it. It's illegitimate suffering." I have never seen a cold disappear so fast. Before that service was over, he had no more sniffles, and his throat had cleared up.

It pays to know Scripture!

❏ *Number Two: Constantly giving in to fleshly lusts*

> Do not be deceived: God cannot be mocked. A man reaps what he sows.
>
> The one who sows to please his sinful nature, from that nature will reap destruction; the one who sows to please the Spirit, from the Spirit will reap eternal life.
>
> —Galatians 6:7-8

When you give in to fleshly desires, you become a sickness magnet.

• If a person is sexually promiscuous, he or she will likely catch a disease.

• If you overeat or eat the wrong things, you can invite heart disease, diabetes, high blood pressure, or a host of other problems.

• If you don't exercise and give in to laziness or lack of discipline, you shorten your life.

• If you give in to the desire to stay up late and sleep the wrong hours, you can lower your immune system's ability to fight off viruses.

The good news is that the Bible says there is no temptation we face that is unique, and God always provides an escape hatch.

My advice is to use it! Avoid those fleshly lusts whether sexual, gluttonous, or lazy, and you will keep your health on track.

❒ *Number Three: Violating legitimate rules*

Every now and then I get letters from people trying to persuade me to become an anti-government preacher. They have all sorts of Scriptures (taken out of context) as to why Christians should be against the government.

> Everyone must submit himself to the governing authorities, for there is no authority except that which God has established. The authorities that exist have been established by God.
>
> Consequently, he who rebels against the authority is rebelling against what God has instituted, and those who do so will bring judgment on themselves.
>
> For rulers hold no terror for those who do right, but for those who do wrong. Do you want to be free from fear of the one in authority? Then do what is right and he will commend you.
>
> For he is God's servant to do you good. But if you do wrong, be afraid, for he does not bear the sword for nothing. He is God's servant, an agent of wrath to bring punishment on the wrongdoer.

> Therefore, it is necessary to submit to the authorities, not only because of possible punishment but also because of conscience.
>
> This is also why you pay taxes, for the authorities are God's servants, who give their full time to governing.
>
> Give everyone what you owe him: If you owe taxes, pay taxes; if revenue, then revenue; if respect, then respect; if honor, then honor.
>
> —Romans 13:1-7

I find that people who are against authority or who bristle about the rules that govern them are prime candidates for sickness. The Bible says we should obey the government and powers over us because they were put there by God. But some Christians say, "The only rules I'm going to obey are the Bible rules." These people have a rebellious, independent spirit that sooner or later gets them into trouble.

Sometimes they end up spurning the advice of a doctor or a friend. They become bullheaded about their eating or exercise habits (or lack of exercise). They even drive away friends and potential spouses because they have a chip on their shoulder. Medical studies show that people who are happily married live longer and healthier lives. How do you find a mate when you are constantly complaining?

Philippians 2:14 says:

> Do everything without complaining or arguing.

Proverbs 15:4a says:

> The tongue that brings healing is a tree of life...

Doctors also now know that discouragement and prolonged sadness lead to illnesses such as heart disease. Our attitude and our physical health are intricately intertwined. If you are a rule-breaker in one area of life, chances are it will cause you to have poor health.

❑ *Number Four: Failing to honor all men*

> Show proper respect to everyone: Love the brotherhood of believers, fear God, honor the king.
>
> —1 Peter 2:17

All people, even the most grievous sinners, deserve to be treated with dignity.

I heard about a Christian speaker who was flying into Tulsa, Oklahoma, and the driver meeting him at the airport was five minutes late because of a funeral. When the speaker got into the car, he severely reprimanded the driver then minutes later got in front of the television cameras and was all smiles.

That man failed to honor the driver. He didn't even treat him like a person.

We had an old drunk named Leon in our neighborhood, and we always treated him well, though he had many problems. We even bought him gifts for Christmas. He would often stand outside and ask Mary Jo for a cup of coffee, and she would give it to him. Many times I prayed with Leon in the driveway as he cried and repented, though it never seemed to change him.

But I remember, like it was yesterday, the day I gave an altar call, and there was Leon at the altar accepting the invitation. He finally became a true believer.

There is something about honoring people that will bless your life and keep you from sickness. The Bible says that if you honor your father and mother, you will have long life and things will go well with you. That means God will maintain your health.

> "Honor your father and your mother, so that you may live long in the land the LORD your God is giving you.
>
> —Exodus 20:12
>
> "Honor your father and mother"—which is the first commandment with a promise.
>
> —Ephesians 6:2

I remember praying, "Lord, how do I honor my father who has been dead for a long time?" The Lord dropped these words into my heart: "Honor your father by honoring your father's sister." I have one living relative on my father's side, so I began honoring her by sending cards on special days and letting her know I cared about her.

When you honor other people, you bring the blessing of God on your health. I believe He protects us from illness and injury when we show honor, not just to our parents, but to all people.

◻ *Number Five: Failing to walk in love toward believers*

I often encounter people whose entire "ministry" is to say who's in the body of Christ and who isn't. They are like watchdogs who bark at anything.

The Bible says we are not to judge another man's servant. If a person tells you he is born again and loves Jesus, what right do you have to sit in judgment over him? Let God judge him. If you suspect that he's in error somehow, remember that Elijah was a heretic at one time. So was Job. So was the Apostle Paul. So even were the twelve disciples. Read their theology — God had to correct all of them. Nobody is totally pure in his or her doctrine on peripheral issues, but God looks at the sincerity of the heart.

Every person has a different perspective or set of gifts that make him unique. The prophets in the Bible had different personalities that showed in their writing. It isn't for us to say who's in and who's out of the family of God. Jesus said that weeds and wheat — the true and the false — grow together but don't try to pluck the weeds because you may accidentally pluck wheat. I have seen books and ministries do great damage to the Body of Christ by saying that certain preachers or movements are heretical and should be rejected.

> Jesus told them another parable: "The kingdom of heaven is like a man who sowed good seed in his field.
>
> But while everyone was sleeping, his enemy came and sowed weeds among the wheat, and went away.
>
> When the wheat sprouted and formed heads, then the weeds also appeared.
>
> "The owner's servants came to him and said, 'Sir, didn't you sow good seed in your field? Where then did the weeds come from?'
>
> "'An enemy did this,' he replied. "The servants asked him, 'Do you want us to go and pull them up?'
>
> "'No,' he answered, 'because while you are pulling the weeds, you may root up the wheat with them.
>
> Let both grow together until the harvest. At that time I will tell the harvesters: First collect the weeds and tie them in bundles to be burned; then gather the wheat and bring it into my barn.'"
>
> —Matthew 13:24-30

He answered, "The one who sowed the good seed is the Son of Man.

The field is the world, and the good seed stands for the sons of the kingdom. The weeds are the sons of the evil one, and the enemy who sows them is the devil. The harvest is the end of the age, and the harvesters are angels.

"As the weeds are pulled up and burned in the fire, so it will be at the end of the age.

The Son of Man will send out his angels, and they will weed out of his kingdom everything that causes sin and all who do evil.

They will throw them into the fiery furnace, where there will be weeping and gnashing of teeth.

Then the righteous will shine like the sun in the kingdom of their Father. He who has ears, let him hear.

—Matthew 13:37-43

Robert Schuller has taken his share of criticism. I went to the Crystal Cathedral many years ago and felt a little cautious because we had heard that he did not preach the Gospel. To this day I differ with Schuller on certain issues of eschatology. But that day I visited his church, I heard the Gospel of Jesus Christ, the blood of Jesus Christ, and that the way to Heaven was through Jesus Christ alone. I realized that Schuller had been unfairly criticized.

Walking in love will bring the blessing of health.

❏ *Number Six: Failing to honor God*

Blessed are all who fear the LORD, who walk in His ways.

> You will eat the fruit of your labor; blessings and prosperity will be yours.

—Psalm 128:2

I had a friend who was not committed to God and didn't come to church. I kept him as a friend, without hanging around him much, because I believe that a true friend leads you closer to God at all times. Still, I didn't want to cut him off. I thought maybe my example would help him to be a more consistent Christian.

Whenever he wanted attention, he would call and say, "I'm having a heart attack. Please come, and see me." That worked for the first few times, but then I realized he just wanted attention, so I stopped going.

One night I received a call that he was back in the hospital, so Mary Jo and I waited a few days and then went to visit. I couldn't believe what I saw in that hospital bed: an emaciated man with sunken eyes who weighed probably less than ninety pounds. This time, he was serious.

I prayed for him. He lifted his hands and said, "Father, please heal me," but a few hours later he died. He had not honored God with his life. He had cried "wolf" to me and probably had done the same thing to God, making promises he didn't intend to keep. When the crisis came, he had no faith to stand on and no credibility with God, or man.

When we honor God, we can call on His Name and expect to be healed. He will be right at our side. He will know we are sincere and will raise us up for continued service.

Feelings are not the thermometer we should use to determine our potential for healing.

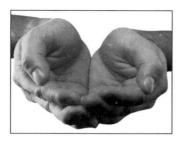

Chapter Seven

Twenty-Five Helps For Radical Healing

The next few chapters contain the most practical advice you will ever receive on healing. I call them Helps For Healing, but they are by no means a doctrine or a secret process. Rather, they are a checklist for you or someone you love to consider as you pray for healing in your own body.

After following these twenty-five steps, you will have the faith to be healed and the knowledge to push aside hindrances to healing.

❏ *1. Don't deny the reality of sickness.*

Every year, it seems, headlines tell us that another child has died because his or her parents refused to seek medical treatment because of their religious beliefs. That's not faith; that's denial.

Divine healing is not about denying the truth. Mind-science cults deny the existence of sickness claiming that it is a figment of the imagination. But Jesus doesn't tell us to deny reality.

I know a lady who had a tumor on her face that everybody could see was getting bigger, but she decided to deny that it was there and didn't seek treatment.

Paul didn't deny reality. He said frankly, "We are troubled on every side." Even Jesus said, "My soul is overwhelmed with sorrow to the point of death" (Matthew 26:38). Christians don't deny the reality of sickness — but we know the Answer.

❑ *2. Don't focus on the sickness but on the promise of God.*

I call this the right side of the "but." Paul said he was "persecuted, *but* not abandoned" (2 Corinthians 4:9). The psalmist said, "A righteous man may have many troubles, *but* the Lord delivers him from them all" (Psalm 34:19). The focus is always on the right side which is the side of the promise of God. Yes, I may be sick, *but* by His stripes I am healed. The doctors may say I don't have long to live, *but* Jesus bore my infirmities. Focus on the right side of the "but" for good health.

❏ *3. Speak what you believe.*

A lady who had suffered a stroke came to a healing service. She was numb on her left side, and when we prayed for her, nothing happened. She felt no different when she left the altar. She went back to her seat, and somebody said, "Did you feel anything?" She said, "No, but God is beginning a healing in me."

On the way home, she felt a tingle in her hand where she had previously had no feeling. She told her husband, "My healing is beginning to manifest." By the time they got home, she was totally healed, mobile, and all the numbness was gone.

Feelings are not the thermometer we should use to determine our potential for healing. It's the defeated, unstable Christian who constantly asks, "Do I feel that God can heal me?" The person on the path to healing speaks words of faith regardless of feelings.

When we are sick, we must put our trust in the Bible which says without a shadow of doubt that we will be healed.

Paul said in 2 Corinthians 5:7, "We live by faith, not by sight." Many times I will pray for somebody, and they will say, "I didn't feel anything." Faith is not a feeling. Faith is standing on what God said. Speak what you believe not what you feel.

❐   *4. Listen to the right friends.*

The right friends and the right church will encourage you to seek healing. Job had three friends who gave him the wrong advice and blamed him for his problems. None of them suggested that the devil might be the culprit. They represented the kind of people who look for answers in the wrong places.

We need a friend who will speak from God's Word, not his own opinion, and will fight with us against the enemy. Don't quit because of self-styled advisors who tell you healing is not for today or not for you. The right friends see the miracle around the corner.

❐   *5. Know that sickness should not last a long time.*

Sickness should not be an ongoing condition for the believer. Paul said his affliction was light and momentary. Peter said that after you have suffered a while, you will be made perfect (1 Peter 5:10 KJV). Don't accept ongoing sickness as your lot in life, but let faith rise up to believe that you can be free.

❐   *6. Keep acute spiritual vision.*

It's hard to stay spiritual when your back is aching or you're too weak to get up, but we are called to look not at the things which are seen but at the things which are not seen, for the things which are seen are temporal, but the things which are not seen are eternal.

Paul never lost his spiritual vision during times of adversity. He saw through to the other side of the affliction. You and I should do the same.

☐ *7. Don't view healing as magic or luck.*

Some Christians treat prayer like a slot machine. "If I could just get the splinter from the Cross, I'll have a miracle." Or, "This might be my lucky day! I'm going to go to church, and maybe I'll get healed."

Healing is neither magic nor luck. It's simply a matter of God's love responding to our faith. Cults and charlatans promote mind-healing, but when God heals, it's not mind-healing but divine healing!

I still remember the day they brought a sixty-pound woman into church, so thin she looked like a little girl. Cancer had eaten up her body. She was a precious Catholic lady and had tried pilgrimages and relics to be healed, but nothing worked. She heard about our church and had her brother and husband bring her to a service the day after she was released from the hospital to go home and die. (When they opened her up, she was so full of cancer they didn't bother sewing her shut but put butterfly bandages on her.)

One of the ministers laid hands on her and had to turn his head away because there was such a foul odor of death about her. He said, "Jesus, please heal her." She collapsed as if she were dead. Her husband started crying, thinking she had died; the brother was having a fit. The pastor said, "Leave her there. It might be the power of God on her."

Soon she started breathing heavily and then laughing. She said, "I haven't been able to breathe like this in months!" Under her own power, she stood up smiling and said, "I felt heat go all over my body up and down. I think God healed me!"

Her husband took her home, still wondering what had happened. Within a few days, she was up to ninety pounds. Within a few weeks, she was up to her ideal weight. Her specialist ran a battery of tests and declared her cancer-free! Her story even made it into the newspaper, and her healing became contagious!

Healing miracles are not like a slot machine. We can trust God 100 percent of the time when we put our faith in Him.

❑ *8. Give up grudges.*

Francis McNutt was a born-again Catholic priest. A lady who was not able to have children visited him and said, "I've hated my dad for years because he sexually abused me when I was a child, and I have never been able to forgive him. Will you help me?" He prayed with her, and she was released from her grudge. Nine months later she had a baby. That unforgiveness had defiled her body, and she never would have been healed if she hadn't forgiven.

> Therefore I tell you, whatever you ask for in prayer, believe that you have received it, and it will be yours. And when you stand praying, if you hold anything against anyone, forgive him, so that your Father in heaven may forgive you your sins.
>
> —Mark 11:24-25
>
> See to it that no one misses the grace of God and that no bitter root grows up to cause trouble and defile many.
>
> —Hebrews 12:15

Grudges and unforgiveness may be one of the most powerful hindrances to healing, second only to unbelief. You will be amazed at what power flows in your life when you are 100 percent grudge-free!

Criticizing anointed servants of God is a way to open the door to ill health.

Chapter Eight

Helps For Radical Healing, Part II

☐ *9. Take care of your body.*

Some people get healed then slide back into the same problem because they don't take good care of their bodies. Laziness, lack of exercise, overwork, along with poor eating and sleeping habits all lead to poor health. What good is divine intervention if we don't care for our physical temples?

> Don't you know that you yourselves are God's temple and that God's Spirit lives in you?
>
> If anyone destroys God's temple, God will destroy him; for God's temple is sacred, and you are that temple.
>
> —1 Corinthians 3:16-17

Some people overwork so they can have the car or home they've always wanted. Then they wonder why their body breaks down a few years later.

Some people get healed and then go on eating binges. You don't have to be a nutritionist to know that fast food and candy bars will wear your body out and make you sluggish and flabby.

Don't expect God to repeatedly rescue you from problems caused by gluttony! Do all you can to care for your body, and then pray for healing.

☐ *10. Kick the fear-and-worry habit.*

Fear has a strange way of attracting the wrong results. Job had a dreaded disease and said, "The thing that I greatly feared has come upon me." Dr. W.C. Alvarez, who used to be at the Mayo Clinic in Minnesota, said hospitals would clear out if people would quit worrying. Dr. Russell Cecil, a world recognized authority on arthritis, said worry is among the chief causes of rheumatism, bursitis, and arthritis.

> So my counsel is: Don't worry about *things*—food, drink, and clothes. For you already have life and a body—and they are far more important than what to eat and wear.
>
> Look at the birds! They don't worry about what to eat—they don't need to sow or reap or store up food—for your heavenly Father feeds them.

And you are far more valuable to him than they are.

Will all your worries add a single moment to your life?

And why worry about your clothes? Look at the field lilies! They don't worry about theirs.

Yet King Solomon in all his glory was not clothed as beautifully as they.

And if God cares so wonderfully for flowers that are here today and gone tomorrow, won't he more surely care for you, O men of little faith?

So don't worry at all about having enough food and clothing. Why be like the heathen? For they take pride in all these things and are deeply concerned about them. But your heavenly Father already knows perfectly well that you need them, and he will give them to you if you give him first place in your life and live as he wants you to.

So don't be anxious about tomorrow. God will take care of your tomorrow too. Live one day at a time.

—Matthew 6:25-34 (TLB)

Fear not, little flock; for it is your Father's good pleasure to give you the kingdom.

—Luke 12:32 (KJV)

Men's hearts failing them for fear, and for looking after those things which are coming on the earth: for the powers of heaven shall be shaken.

—Luke 21:26 (KJV)

For you did not receive a spirit that makes you a slave again to fear, but you received the Spirit of sonship. And by him we cry, "Abba, Father."

—Romans 8:15

For God hath not given us the spirit of fear; but of power, and of love, and of a sound mind.

—2 Timothy 1:7 (KJV)

There is no fear in love. But perfect love drives out fear, because fear has to do with punishment. The one who fears is not made perfect in love.

—1 John 4:18

Even though I walk through the valley of the shadow of death, I will fear no evil, for you are with me; your rod and your staff, they comfort me.

—Psalm 23:4

The LORD is my light and my salvation— whom shall I fear? The LORD is the stronghold of my life— of whom shall I be afraid?

When evil men advance against me to devour my flesh, when my enemies and my foes attack me, they will stumble and fall.

Though an army besiege me, my heart will not fear; though war break out against me, even then will I be confident.

—Psalm 27:1-3

How true is the saying, "I was worried sick." But the joy of the Lord is our strength!

❏   **11. Understand the Lord's Body during Holy Communion.**

Paul wrote:

> A man ought to examine himself before he eats of the bread and drinks of the cup. For anyone who eats and drinks without recognizing the body of the Lord eats and drinks judgment on himself. That is why many among you are weak and sick, and a number of you have fallen asleep.
>
> —1 Corinthians 11:28-30

That means people die before their time when they don't approach communion with reverence and purify their hearts before receiving it. Can this happen today? Absolutely!

Approach the table of the Lord with sincerity, reverence, holiness, and childlike faith, and you will guard against illness.

❏   **12. Speak well of God's anointed servants.**

Miriam, Moses' older sister, was a prophetess, a dancer, a musician, and a songwriter. But God, instead, had anointed Moses to deliver the children of Israel out of Egypt, and the Word says, "Touch not my anointed, and do my prophets no harm."

Miriam thought she could do just as well as Moses, so she told the people, "I hear from God just as much as Moses does." Suddenly she was afflicted with leprosy. God's protection was removed from her because she denigrated an anointed servant of God.

I have seen this happen in my own lifetime at least two dozen times. One time there were two women in my church who were gossipers, and one was in a position of leadership. People would call her to co-ordinate things, and she would say, "Dave Williams isn't all he's cracked up to be. He's got feet of clay just like everybody else." I found out about it and had a chat with the woman, and she went on the at-tack. "Who do you think you are, trying to run the church?" she said. I told her she would have to give up her leadership position, and she promptly left the church.

Within two days, she had a serious accident, and her body would not heal. Doctors were amazed. They tried experimental drugs, but to this day, she still has not healed.

The other lady, who had been a relentless gos-siper, was gripped by an illness that kept her in ter-rible pain. I confronted her about the gossip, and she broke down and repented. God healed her, and she has been a humble member of the church ever since.

Criticizing anointed servants is a way to open the door to ill health. Maybe you bad-mouth your pastor, or associate pastor, or a television preacher. God's servants are not perfect, but they are to be honored.

> *Saying,* Touch not mine anointed, and do my prophets no harm.
>
> —Psalm 105:15 (KJV)

If you want your soul to be fat and flow over into healing, be diligent about reading the Word of God.

Chapter Nine

Helps For Radical Healing, Part III

☐ *13. Read the Bible to build faith.*

It amazes me the number of times I visit someone in their hospital room, and they are watching soap operas! What are they meditating on? God didn't send *General Hospital* or *As the World Turns* to heal them. Psalm 107:20a says He sent His Word and healed them.

People don't get into the Word because they are sluggards. The soul of the sluggard desires and has nothing. But Proverbs 13:4b says:

> ... the desires of the diligent are fully satisfied.

If you want your soul to be fat and flow over into healing, be diligent about reading the Word to build faith.

> So then faith *cometh* by hearing, and hearing by
> the word of God.
>
> —Romans 10:17 (KJV)

❐ 14. Resist the devil.

Some believe that sickness is normal. I say, if anything has the ability to steal my health, it is satanic in
nature. Jesus said:

> The thief comes only to steal and kill and de-
> stroy; I have come that they may have life, and
> have it to the full.
>
> —John 10:10

When your health has been stolen, it's hard to have
an abundant life. How do we keep the devourer
away? James said:

> Submit yourselves, then, to God. Resist the devil,
> and he will flee from you.
>
> —James 4:7

Peter put it this way:

> Resist him [the devil], standing firm in the faith,
> because you know that your brothers through-
> out the world are undergoing the same kind of
> sufferings.
>
> —1 Peter 5:9 (Brackets Added)

Too many people play the devil's games. For instance, the news might say it's flu season, so we go
to the drugstore and stock up on medicine just in
case we come down with the flu. We make provision
for Satan to attack!

I have never understood why employers give people sick days — that's like saying we expect you to get sick twelve days a year.

Before I was a pastor, I worked at the power company and told my co-workers, "I believe in divine health. God is going to keep me healthy." After I said that, I wondered if I should have! I knew the devil would challenge me. That very week, I got up and was dizzy, light-headed, sweating, and had aches and chills. My stomach was nauseated, and I had that sick taste in my mouth. I didn't want to get out from under the covers, but I had to go to work. My first thought was, "I'm going to have to call in sick." Then I remembered that I had said that God would keep me in good health. I had to treat it as an attack from the devil.

I was shaking with chills as I combed my hair, washed my face, and shaved. All the while I was saying, "In the Name of Jesus, by His stripes, I am healed. Devil, I resist you steadfastly in the faith."

I got in the car — sweating, my head spinning. I thought I was going to have to pull over because I felt so weak and dizzy, but I kept confessing the Word all the way to work. People passing me must have thought I was crazy because I kept yelling at someone they could not see.

I pulled into the parking lot, walked up the steps, and when I walked through the door, I noticed something. I felt well! The fever was gone, and no one ever knew how sick I had been. By the time I got to my station, I was ready for anything.

When I left the power company, I asked the secretary how many sick days I had taken. She looked in the book, her eyes got big, and she said, "You've never taken a sick day."

In all my years of being a pastor, I can think of only one time I turned the pulpit over to someone else because I was not able to preach, and that was after I had shoulder surgery.

Resist the devil, and he *will* flee from you!

Chapter Ten

Helps For Radical Healing, Part IV

☐ *15. Understand God's will concerning healing.*

We spent a chapter on this earlier in the book. To be healed, you must believe that God wants to heal you. There is no greater hindrance than your own unbelief, so you must overcome it, like the man who said:

> "I do believe; help me overcome my unbelief!"
>
> —Mark 9:24b

Chuck Smith was pastoring in Tucson, Arizona, when a lady came to him, hysterical. Her son had torn his finger off in a baseball accident. Chuck went to the hospital, laid his hands on the little boy, and prayed a prayer of faith. Even in his own mind, he wasn't convinced the boy would be healed. But the boy believed that his finger was going to grow back, even though the doctor said it was impossible.

The boy went home, and the finger grew half an inch. The mother took him back to the doctor who said, "This happens sometimes. There is an appearance of growth, but it will never grow to be a normal finger."

A few months went by, and the finger grew out another half inch. The doctor took pictures of it because by this time it was making medical history, but he said, "Because the finger was torn off below the fingernail, there's nothing in there to manufacture a fingernail. There will never be a fingernail on that finger."

The finger continued to grow and developed a fingernail. To this day you can't tell where the boy's finger was torn off in the accident.

That never would have happened if the boy disbelieved God, but he had been taught that God heals. He understood how God works.

❑   *16. Speak faith words about your health.*

Proverbs 15:4 (KJV) says:

> A wholesome tongue *is* a tree of life: but perverseness therein *is* a breach in the spirit.

When we speak something other than God's Word, that is perversity. It causes a tear in our spirit, so when He pours healing in, it runs right out of us. For healing to overflow into the mind and the body, our spirit must be able to hold it.

Ask some people, "How are you doing?" and you will regret it. They will give you a long list of their ailments. Jesus said we are going to be judged for our idle words. James said if you can control your tongue, you can control your whole body.

> We all stumble in many ways. If anyone is never at fault in what he says, he is a perfect man, able to keep his whole body in check.
>
> When we put bits into the mouths of horses to make them obey us, we can turn the whole animal.
>
> Or take ships as an example. Although they are so large and are driven by strong winds, they are steered by a very small rudder wherever the pilot wants to go.
>
> Likewise the tongue is a small part of the body, but it makes great boasts. Consider what a great forest is set on fire by a small spark.
>
> The tongue also is a fire, a world of evil among the parts of the body. It corrupts the whole person, sets the whole course of his life on fire, and is itself set on fire by hell.
>
> All kinds of animals, birds, reptiles and creatures of the sea are being tamed and have been tamed by man, but no man can tame the tongue. It is a restless evil, full of deadly poison.

> With the tongue we praise our Lord and Father,
> and with it we curse men, who have been made
> in God's likeness.
>
> Out of the same mouth come praise and curs-
> ing. My brothers, this should not be.
>
> —James 3:2-10

It is easy to swim downstream with everybody else, speaking negatively and letting so-called "common sense" rule our minds. But the Bible says to speak against common sense with heavenly truth, "Let the weak say I am strong." There is a difference between the facts and the truth. When we confess the truth, it overtakes the facts.

> The tongue has the power of life and death, and
> those who love it will eat its fruit.
>
> —Proverbs 18:21

☐ 17. *Look to Christ not the method or messenger.*

Jesus is the Healer. Whenever we look to a man or a method, we run into problems.

I remember a man back in 1982 who called the church and requested that the pastor visit him in the hospital. He was cranky and only came to church once every three months or so. But when he had a problem, he wanted the "head honcho" not any "second rates." He demanded that I, the senior pastor, come and visit him. So I went. I talked to him for ten minutes, and he griped, complained, and whined. I prayed for him, left, and he died. I asked God why he died, and the Lord said it was because he was looking for a healing messenger instead of the healing Christ.

Richard, a member of my church, injured his back and was in bed for almost a year. The finances were draining. He couldn't work. His daughter attended children's church and learned about praying for the sick with the laying on of hands. She went home and said, "Daddy, your back has been hurting for so long. Can I pray for it?" She put her little hands on his back and said, "God, please heal Daddy in Jesus' Name." Richard got off the bed, totally healed, and went back to work the next week. He came to church and was practically doing cartwheels; he was so excited.

It's not the messenger that heals us; it's the healing Christ!

When you are specific, you will rejoice knowing that God healed your problem as a result of prayer.

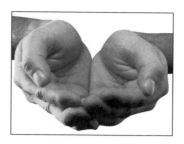

Chapter Eleven

Helps For Radical Healing, Part V

❑ *18. No one is unworthy of being healed.*

Back in the 1970s, our church sent a group to Chrysler Arena in Ann Arbor for a Kathryn Kuhlman crusade. One lady who signed up to go was a barmaid who had cancer. She was in line smoking a cigarette waiting for the crusade to begin. No sooner did we get into the service then Kuhlman said, "Somebody over here has been healed of cancer." That barmaid stood up and went up for prayer, and the next week the doctors found not a bit of cancer in her body.

Jesus doesn't heal on the basis of our being worthy. He heals on the basis of His character. His character is to heal. When the ten lepers came to Jesus, He didn't say, "Five of you are worthy, and five of you aren't." He healed all ten.

I believe that the vast majority of people who don't get healed feel there is something wrong in their lives and can't believe in God's healing. It is harder for Christians to be healed than for sinners sometimes because we have encountered a holy God and don't feel worthy. That's the time to say, "He is my only righteousness. I am made acceptable to the Father through Jesus!" We are worthy because He is worthy!

> But God demonstrates his own love for us in this: While we were still sinners, Christ died for us.
>
> —Romans 5:8

❒ 19. Don't attach a false value to sickness.

Some think God uses sickness and disease to make them more righteous or holy, but there's not one verse of Scripture, from Genesis through Revelation, that suggests that God uses sickness and disease to teach His people — persecution, yes; illness, never.

Interjecting human thinking into God's Word is how we have gotten so messed up in our understanding. God gets glory in *healing* not sickness!

I know of only one case in the New Testament where God used sickness to teach a lesson, and that was the man who was committing incest and professing to be a believer. Paul said in 1 Corinthians 5:5, "Hand this man over to Satan, so that the sinful nature may be destroyed and his spirit saved on the day of the Lord." God removed His protection and allowed Satan to bring sickness on him, so that he might come to the place of repentance.

That is not the same as being sick for God's sake which should never be part of a Christian's life.

☐ *20. Pray specifically.*

> Therefore I tell you, whatever you ask for in prayer, believe that you have received it, and it will be yours.
>
> —Mark 11:24

Prayer power increases when we pray specifically for a need. If someone has a mental illness, pray for the mind. If someone has a demonic influence, pray for deliverance. If someone has a virus, pray against it.

When you are specific, you will rejoice knowing that God healed your problem as a result of prayer.

☐ *21. No problem is too complicated or too simple to bother God with.*

My dear aunt came to one of our healing meetings. She had something wrong with her and had been complaining about it for a long time. The power of

God was moving mightily, and she came up and said, "I don't want prayer because there are so many people so much worse than me."

We have the mentality that there's only so much healing to go around. The fact is, there is enough healing to go around for every man, woman, boy, and girl on planet Earth, and for your dog too!

Some people think, "All I have is a plantar's wart," or acne, or hangnails. God is concerned about your problem regardless of how little you think it is. Matthew 4:23 says:

> Jesus went throughout Galilee, teaching in their synagogues, preaching the good news of the kingdom, and healing every disease and sickness among the people.

"Every disease" means: allergies, migraine headaches, ingrown toenails, acid reflux, bruised thumbs — any ailment. Nothing is too small for Him to touch.

❐ 22. Desire the healing.

A man came to my office one day with a tray that contained twenty-five brown pill bottles. He said, "These are all the pills I'm taking. Doc's got me on this one, this one ..." He told me what each one was for and showed me the charts of when he took them during the day. I asked if he would like prayer, and he said, "No, I've got it all taken care of right here."

He didn't want to be healed; he wanted to show off his pill collection!

Jesus said:

> Therefore I tell you, whatever you ask for in prayer, believe that you have received it, and it will be yours.

> —Mark 11:24

Proverbs 10:24b (KJV) says:

> ... the desire of the righteous shall be granted.

Without desire, it's like praying with the brakes on.

Some people don't desire to be healed. They desire the disability check. They desire sympathy. You see them week after week. They never confess the Word of God but always confess their problem. "I have to take seven different kinds of medication in order to stay alive. Want to hear about them?"

I knew a blind man, and I used to take him places because he said he wanted to "see" them. One day he asked if I would take him to the radio station, and on the way over he said, "I know what I'm going to do. I'm going to get them to feel sorry for me because I'm blind, and maybe they'll give me some records." I took him around the radio station and introduced him to the disc jockey. My blind friend said, "I'm blind, but I sure love music." The disc jockey gave him loads of records. We walked out, and my friend was all smiles. He said, "Being blind sure has its advantages."

Chapter Twelve

Helps For Radical Healing, Part VI

❐ *23. Be tenacious.*

Some people receive prayer once and think it didn't work. A man in Lansing had a disease and heard about Mount Hope Church. We were in five services at that time. He came to the 8 o'clock service and got prayed for but wasn't healed. He came to the 9:30 service, got prayed for, but wasn't healed. He came to the 11:30 service, got prayed for, but wasn't healed. He came back at 5 o'clock for the Sunday night service, got prayed for, but wasn't healed. He came back at 7 o'clock for the Sunday night service, got prayed for, and God healed him. He didn't stop coming until he got what he came for!

He was like Jacob grabbing the thigh of God saying, "I'm not going to let you go until you bless me."

Sometimes we need to get determined. When we are sick we need to say, "I'm not going to let You go until I get this healing manifested in my body."

Smith Wigglesworth would lock himself in a room and not come out until he was healed of what ailed him.

A lady with a severed spinal cord came to a service one time and received prayer. Nothing happened. She came to six more services and in the seventh got up out of her wheelchair. A creative miracle had taken place in her body.

A woman in my congregation, named Ruby, was going blind when her boyfriend talked her into coming to our church. She came and was prayed for, and God healed her of blindness. She told me, "I was blind but now I can see." I thought she was quoting "*Amazing Grace,*" but she told me, "I really was blind, and now I can see." I said, "Bring me a letter from your doctor." The next week I received a letter from her doctor that told me what this woman had experienced, and it said it was nothing short of a miracle.

Mary Jo and I were in a meeting in Detroit, Michigan, and the first night they wheeled a little lady in. Her legs looked like toothpicks, no bigger around than a quarter. I remember thinking, "Even if she's healed, there's no way she can walk on those things. They'll snap."

During the fourth meeting, the evangelist commanded, "Sister, in the Name of Jesus, rise up and walk." I thought, "Don't say that! Have you seen her legs?" She stood up in the wheelchair, and the place went wild, and she started walking. The next night I thought, "I'll be surprised if she's walking when we go back to the meeting." I looked, and right next to me was that lady standing, no wheelchair! I was speechless. It was a miracle!

Sometimes it doesn't happen the first time, the second time, or third time, but if you hang in there, it will.

❐ *24. Accept professional help as a legitimate means of God's healing.*

I had a piece of skin growing near my eye one time. It didn't hurt or itch, but it looked ugly. I prayed about it, and I believed God for healing, but I couldn't get it to go away, so I went to the doctor. He looked at it and said, "That's nothing," grabbed a razor blade, and cut if off!

Would God have gotten more glory if I had kept praying until it disappeared? I don't think so.

There are two extremes: there are those who run to the doctor for everything, no matter what it is. I call them "sickbay commandos." And the other extreme are those who don't go to doctors for anything, take no vitamins, and pay no attention to nutritional advice.

I get five medical newsletters every month to increase my knowledge of health. I take vitamins and other supplements. I want to do everything I can to keep myself healthy.

As our church added services to our Sunday schedule, it began to affect me physically. On Monday mornings my legs would hurt terribly from standing and walking all day Sunday. I read about another pastor who held five services on Sunday and on Monday would wrap an electric blanket around his legs and stay in bed all day because of the pain.

I didn't tell anybody I was hurting, but some of the men on staff saw me rubbing my legs one day and suggested I try arch supports, which I did, and within a few days the pain was gone.

Don't ignore the value of professional help or good advice when you need it!

❑   *25. Believe that faith is always now.*

Hebrews 11:1 says, "*Now* faith is" — not tomorrow but now. That means faith only exists in the present moment — right now. It can't be scheduled for next Tuesday or when the healing evangelist comes. If you are to be healed, you must believe *now!*

A businessman who had multiple sclerosis came to our healing school. He normally attended a Methodist church but had already lost the use of his right arm and wanted to be healed. He listened every day for five days, and on the last day I had the students lay hands on people and pray for them. Everyone who wanted healing was told, "When they lay hands on you, believe that you will recover. The Bible doesn't say that a miracle will happen immediately but that the sick shall recover."

> And these signs will accompany those who believe: In my name they will drive out demons; they will speak in new tongues; they will pick up snakes with their hands; and when they drink deadly poison, it will not hurt them at all; they will place their hands on sick people, and they will get well."
>
> —Mark 16:17-18

The businessman received prayer and believed that he would recover but still had no control over his arm and fingers. He didn't concede defeat but said,

"According to what is promised in the Bible, I am recovering."

He didn't say, "Oh well. I'll wait until next week. Maybe then I'll have faith." He believed right then. His faith was *now*.

The next day he could move his thumb, the day after that his finger, and after a week his whole hand. He called rejoicing, praising the Lord, and said, "So that's how it works!" Doctors said he was in complete remission. I call it complete recovery based on faith in God's Word.

The tendency in many churches is to call it healing only if someone pops immediately out of a wheelchair, but it doesn't always happen that way. Regardless of when or how it happens, faith is always now.

Here's a quick review of the Twenty-Five Helps For Radical Healing:

❒ *1. Don't deny the reality of sickness.*

❒ *2. Don't focus on the sickness but on the promise of God.*

❒ *3. Speak what you believe.*

❒ *4. Listen to the right friends.*

❒ *5. Know that sickness should not last a long time.*

❏   *6. Keep acute spiritual vision.*

❏   *7. Don't view healing as magic or luck.*

❏   *8. Give up grudges.*

❏   *9. Take care of your body.*

❏   *10. Kick the fear-and-worry habit.*

❏   *11. Understand the Lord's Body during Holy Communion.*

❏   *12. Speak well of God's anointed servants.*

❏   *13. Read the Bible to build faith.*

❏   *14. Resist the devil.*

❏   *15. Understand God's will concerning healing.*

❏   *16. Speak faith words about your health.*

❏   *17. Look to Christ not the method or messenger.*

❏   *18. No one is unworthy of being healed.*

❏   *19. Don't attach a false value to sickness.*

❏   *20. Pray specifically.*

❏   *21. No problem is too complicated or too simple to bother God with.*

❏   *22. Desire the healing.*

❐   *23. Be tenacious.*

❐   *24. Accept professional help as a legitimate means of God's healing.*

❐   *25. Believe that faith is always now.*

The Last Word

Don't you want to be well? Don't you want to grasp the promise of healing? God has a wonderful miracle in store for you, and this book is meant to be a gateway for you to receive it.

Now it's your turn. Do you want to be healed? Then stand on the Word of God right now, and be convinced that healing is for you. God will honor your faith as it rises up in you.

You can be radically healed in your living room, your bedroom, or your prayer closet.

You can be radically healed in a church service.

You can be radically healed when the elders anoint you with oil.

You can be radically healed when people from far away pray for you.

But whatever you do — don't give up! Put yourself in the path of a miracle by praying and receiving prayer and believing and speaking the promises of healing in the Bible. As your heart gets in tune with God's truth, your body will have no choice but to follow. Disease will flee. Injuries will heal. You will be protected from sickness. The only contagious thing about you will be your faith!

About The Author

Dave Williams is pastor of Mount Hope Church and International Outreach Ministries, with world headquarters in Lansing, Michigan. He has served for over 20 years, leading the church in Lansing from 226 to over 4000 today. Dave sends trained ministers into unreached cities to establish disciple-making churches, and, as a result, today has "branch" churches in the United States, Philippines, and in Africa.

Dave is the founder and president of Mount Hope Bible Training Institute, a fully accredited institute for training ministers and lay people for the work of the ministry. He has authored over 55 books including the fifteen-time best seller, *The New Life...The Start of Something Wonderful* (with over 2,000,000 books sold), and more recently, *The Miracle Results of Fasting*, *The Road To Radical Riches*, and *Angels*.

The Pacesetter's Path telecast is Dave's weekly television program seen over a syndicated network of secular stations, and nationally over the Sky Angel satellite system. Dave has produced over 125 audio cassette programs including the nationally acclaimed *School of Pacesetting Leadership* which is being used as a training program in churches around the United States, and in Bible Schools in South Africa and the Philippines. He is a popular speaker at conferences, seminars, and conventions. His speaking ministry has taken him across America, Africa, Europe, Asia, and other parts of the world.

Along with his wife, Mary Jo, Dave established The Dave and Mary Jo Williams Charitable Mission (Strategic Global Mission), a mission's ministry for providing scholarships to pioneer pastors and grants to inner-city children's ministries.

Dave's articles and reviews have appeared in national magazines such as *Advance*, *The Pentecostal Evangel*, *Ministries Today*, *The Lansing Magazine*, *The Detroit Free Press* and others. Dave, as a private pilot, flies for fun. He is married, has two grown children, and lives in Delta Township, Michigan.

You may write to Pastor Dave Williams:

P.O. Box 80825

Lansing, MI 48908-0825

Please include your special prayer requests when you write, or you may call the Mount Hope Global Prayer Center: (517) 327-PRAY

DECAPOLIS
PUBLISHING

For a catalog of products, call:

1-517-321-2780 or

1-800-888-7284

or visit us on the web at:

www.mounthopechurch.org

Gilead Healing Center

Gilead
HEALING CENTER

- *The Place Of Another Chance*
- *Training For The Healing Ministry*

- *Prayer*
- *Nutrition*
- *Alternative*
- *Medical*

517-321-2780

We're here for you!
Lansing, Michigan

Books in the "Radical" Series

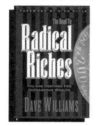 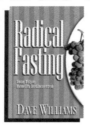  

Radical Riches $19.95

With over 400 power-packed pages you will be on the road
to your financial destiny.

Radical Fasting $9.95

Get ready to be catapulted to new levels of success in your
life, as you discover the triple benefits of *Radical Fasting*.

Radical Healing $9.95

Experience twenty-five keys that will help you to live in
divine health.

Radical Forgiveness (Fall 2003) $9.95

If you have had trouble forgiving, or if you need to realize
afresh the impact that radical forgiveness can have on your
life, then this book is for you.

Quantity Discounts

(Offer good while supplies last)

Radical Riches			Radical Fasting/ Healing/ Forgiveness		
1-9	____	@19.95 ea.			
10-24	____	@17.95 ea.	1-9	____	@9.95 ea.
25-49	____	@15.95 ea.	10-24	____	@7.95 ea.
50-99	____	@13.95 ea.	25-49	____	@6.95 ea.
100-249	____	@10.95 ea.	50-99	____	@5.95 ea.
250-499	____	@8.95 ea.	100-249	____	@4.95 ea.
500+	____	@7.95 ea.	250-499	____	@3.95 ea.
			500+	____	@2.95 ea.

To Order Call:		Write:
517-321-2780	*or*	*The Hope Store*
800-888-7284		*202 South Creyts Road*
		Lansing, Michigan 48917-9284

Please include $4.95 for Shipping and Handling (any size order)

For Your Spiritual Growth

Here's the help you need for your spiritual journey. These books will encourage you, and give you guidance as you seek to draw close to Jesus and learn of Him. Prepare yourself for fantastic growth!

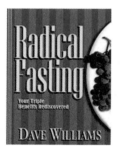

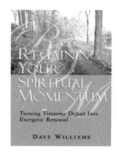

RADICAL FASTING
How would you like to achieve your dreams at "break-neck" speed? Radical fasting may be your key!

REGAINING YOUR SPIRITUAL MOMENTUM
Use this remarkable book as your personal street map to regain your spiritual momentum.

THE JEZEBEL SPIRIT
Do you feel controlled? Learn more about what the Bible says about this manipulating principality's influence.

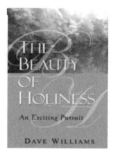

DEVELOPING THE SPIRIT OF A CONQUEROR
Take back what the enemy has stolen from you. Learn how to engage your authority and *Develop the Spirit of a Conqueror*.

BEAUTY OF HOLINESS
We face the choice — holiness or rebellion. True holiness comes about by working together in cooperation with the Holy Spirit.

ABCs OF SUCCESS & HAPPINESS
God wants to give you every good gift, so it's time to accept the responsibility for your success today!

These and other books available from Dave Williams and:

DECAPOLIS PUBLISHING

For Your Spiritual Growth

Here's the help you need for your spiritual journey. These books will encourage you, and give you guidance as you seek to draw close to Jesus and learn of Him. Prepare yourself for fantastic growth!

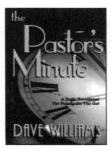

QUESTIONS I HAVE ANSWERED
Get answers to many of the questions you've always wanted to ask a pastor!

THE PASTOR'S MINUTE
A daily devotional for people on the go! Powerful topics will help you grow even when you're in a hurry.

ANGELS: THEY ARE WATCHING YOU!
The Bible tells more than you might think about these powerful beings.

THE WORLD BEYOND
What will Heaven be like? What happens there? Will we see relatives who have gone before us? Who *REALLY* goes to Heaven?

FILLED!
Learn how you can be filled with the mightiest power in the universe. Find out what could be missing from your life.

STRATEGIC GLOBAL MISSION
Read touching stories about God's plan for accelerating the Gospel globally through reaching children and training pastors.

These and other books available from Dave Williams and:

DECAPOLIS PUBLISHING

For Your Spiritual Growth

Here's the help you need for your spiritual journey. These books will encourage you, and give you guidance as you seek to draw close to Jesus and learn of Him. Prepare yourself for fantastic growth!

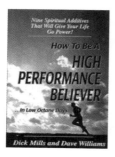

HOW TO BE A HIGH PERFORMANCE BELIEVER
Pour in the nine spiritual additives for real power in your Christian life.

SECRET OF POWER WITH GOD
Tap into the real power with God; the power of prayer. It will change your life!

THE NEW LIFE…
You can get off to a great start on your exciting life with Jesus! Prepare for something wonderful.

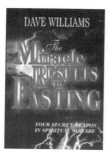

MIRACLE RESULTS OF FASTING
You can receive MIRACLE benefits, spiritually and physically, with this practical Christian discipline.

WHAT TO DO IF YOU MISS THE RAPTURE
If you miss the Rapture, there may still be hope, but you need to follow these clear survival tactics.

THE AIDS PLAGUE
Is there hope? Yes, but only Jesus can bring a total and lasting cure to AIDS.

For Your Spiritual Growth

Here's the help you need for your spiritual journey. These books will encourage you, and give you guidance as you seek to draw close to Jesus and learn of Him. Prepare yourself for fantastic growth!

THE ART OF PACESETTING LEADERSHIP
You can become a successful leader with this proven leadership development course.

GIFTS THAT SHAPE YOUR LIFE
Learn which ministry best fits you, and discover your God-given personality gifts, as well as the gifts of others.

GROWING UP IN OUR FATHER'S FAMILY
You can have a family relationship with your Heavenly Father. Learn how God cares for you.

SUPERNATURAL SOULWINNING
How will we reach our family, friends, and neighbors in this short time before Christ's return?

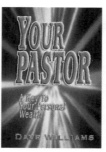

YOUR PASTOR: A KEY TO YOUR PERSONAL WEALTH
By honoring your pastor you can actually be setting yourself up for a financial blessing from God!

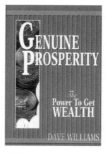

GENUINE PROSPERITY
Learn what it means to be truly prosperous! God gives us the power to get wealth!

These and other books available from Dave Williams and:

DECAPOLIS PUBLISHING

For Your Spiritual Growth

Here's the help you need for your spiritual journey. These books will encourage you, and give you guidance as you seek to draw close to Jesus and learn of Him. Prepare yourself for fantastic growth!

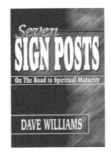

SOMEBODY OUT THERE NEEDS YOU
Along with the gift of salvation comes the great privilege of spreading the gospel of Jesus Christ.

SEVEN SIGNPOSTS TO SPIRITUAL MATURITY
Examine your life to see where you are on the road to spiritual maturity.

THE PASTORS PAY
How much is your pastor worth? Who should set his pay? Discover the scriptural guidelines for paying your pastor.

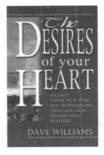

DECEPTION, DELUSION & DESTRUCTION
Recognize spiritual deception and unmask spiritual blindness.

THE ROAD TO RADICAL RICHES
Are you ready to jump from "barely getting by" to God's plan for putting you on the road to Radical Riches?

THE DESIRES OF YOUR HEART
Yes, Jesus wants to give you the desires of your heart, and make them realities.

These and other books available from Dave Williams and:

DECAPOLIS PUBLISHING

For Your Successful Life

These video cassettes will give you successful principles to apply to your whole life. Each a different topic, and each a fantastic teaching of how living by God's Word can give you total success!

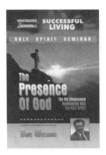

THE PRESENCE OF GOD
Find out how you can have a more dynamic relationship with the Holy Spirit.

FILLED WITH THE HOLY SPIRIT
You can rejoice and share with others in this wonderful experience of God.

GIFTS THAT CHANGE YOUR WORLD
Learn which ministry best fits you, and discover your God-given personality gifts, as well as the gifts of others.

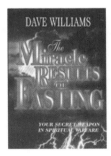

THE SCHOOL OF PACESETTING LEADERSHIP
Leaders are made, not born. You can become a successful leader with this proven leadership development course.

MIRACLE RESULTS OF FASTING
Fasting is your secret weapon in spiritual warfare. Learn how you'll benefit spiritually and physically! Six video messages.

A SPECIAL LADY
If you feel used and abused, this video will show you how you really are in the eyes of Jesus. You are special!

For Your Successful Life

These video cassettes will give you successful principles to apply to your whole life. Each a different topic, and each a fantastic teaching of how living by God's Word can give you total success!

HOW TO BE A HIGH PERFORMANCE BELIEVER
Pour in the nine spiritual additives for real power in your Christian life.

THE UGLY WORMS OF JUDGMENT
Recognizing the decay of judgment in your life is your first step back into God's fullness.

WHAT TO DO WHEN YOU FEEL WEAK AND DEFEATED
Learn about God's plan to bring you out of defeat and into His principles of victory!

WHY SOME ARE NOT HEALED
Discover the obstacles that hold people back from receiving their miracle and how God can help them receive the very best!

BREAKING THE POWER OF POVERTY
The principality of mammon will try to keep you in poverty. Put God FIRST and watch Him bring you into a wealthy place.

HERBS FOR HEALTH
A look at the concerns and fears of modern medicine. Learn the correct ways to open the doors to your healing.

These and other videos available from Dave Williams and:

Running Your Race

These simple but powerful audio cassette singles will help give you the edge you need. Run your race to win!

LONELY IN THE MIDST OF A CROWD
Loneliness is a devastating disease. Learn how to trust and count on others to help.

HERBS FOR HEALTH
A look at the concerns and fears of modern medicine. Learn the correct ways to open the doors to your healing.

HOW TO GET ANYTHING YOU WANT
You can learn the way to get anything you want from God!

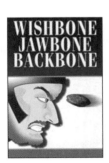

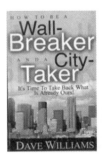

WISHBONE, JAWBONE, BACKBONE
Learn about King David, and how his three "bones" for success can help you in your life quest.

FATAL ENTICEMENTS
Learn how you can avoid the vice-like grip of sin and it's fatal enticements that hold people captive.

HOW TO BE A WALL BREAKER AND A CITY TAKER
You can be a powerful force for advancing the Kingdom of Jesus Christ!

These and other audio tapes available from Dave Williams and:

DECAPOLIS PUBLISHING

Expanding Your Faith

These exciting audio teaching series will help
you to grow and mature in your walk with Christ.
Get ready for amazing new adventures in faith!

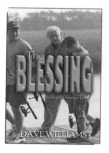

THE BLESSING
Explore the many ways
that God can use you to
bless others, and how
He can correct the
missed blessing.

SIN'S GRIP
Learn how you can avoid
the vice-like grip of sin and
its fatal enticements that
hold people captive.

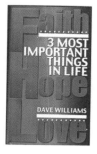

FAITH, HOPE, & LOVE
Listen and let these three
"most important things in
life" change you.

**PSALM 91
THE PROMISE OF
PROTECTION**
Everyone is looking for
protection in these perilous
times. God promises
protection for those who
rest in Him.

**DEVELOPING
THE SPIRIT OF A
CONQUEROR**
You can be a conqueror
through Christ! Also, find
out how to *keep* those
things that you have
conquered.

WHY DO SOME SUFFER
Find out why some people
seem to have suffering in
their lives, and find out
how to avoid it in your life.

**These and other audio tapes
available from Dave Williams and:**

DECAPOLIS
PUBLISHING

Expanding Your Faith

These exciting audio teaching series will help you to grow and mature in your walk with Christ. Get ready for amazing new adventures in faith!

ABCs OF SUCCESS AND HAPPINESS
Learn how to go after God's promises for your life. Happiness and success can be yours today!

FORGIVENESS
The miracle remedy for many of life's problems is found in this basic key for living.

UNTANGLING YOUR TROUBLES
You can be a "trouble untangler" with the help of Jesus!

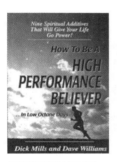

HOW TO BE A HIGH PERFORMANCE BELIEVER
Put in the nine spiritual additives to help run your race and get the prize!

BEING A DISCIPLE AND MAKING DISCIPLES
You can learn to be a "disciple maker" to almost anyone.

HOW TO HELP YOUR PASTOR & CHURCH SUCCEED
You can be an integral part of your church's & pastor's success.

These and other audio tapes available from Dave Williams and:

DECAPOLIS PUBLISHING